A Galaxy of Games

for the Music Class

Margaret Athey

and

Gwen Hotchkiss

Parker Publishing Company, Inc.
West Nyack, New York

Dedicated with affection
and appreciation
to
Brad, Phillip, Karen, Charles,
Chicki, Eric, Lew, and Hotch.

Thanks for your patience and help!

© *1975 by*

Margaret Athey and Gwen Hotchkiss

Library of Congress Cataloging in Publication Data

Athey, Margaret
  A galaxy of games for the music class.

  1. Games with music. 2. Music—Instruction and
study—Juvenile. I. Hotchkiss, Gwen
joint author. II. Title.
MT948.A78   372.8'7'044   75-4889
ISBN 0-13-346064-9

Printed in the United States of America

A WORD FROM THE AUTHORS

"Let's play a game!" What life those words can bring to the dullest of classes. The very nature of music declares that the music class, above all others, should be sparkling with a very special magic. But, alas, such is not always the case. Even the glorious art of music can become humdrum and less than a joy to both teachers and students. To counter such a sad state of affairs, we offer *A Galaxy of Games for the Music Class*.

Not to complicate the teacher's work, for complications exist aplenty; not to create a generation of prize-winners, for we believe that prizes create more problems than they solve; but to add joy and fun to the business of learning music we share these games with you.

May this collection of games bring that special spark of magic to your music classroom.

Margaret Athey
Gwen Hotchkiss

What This Book Will Do For You

If you have any responsibility for teaching music, *A Galaxy of Games for the Music Class* is for you. This is the book that will make your music lessons faster and easier to plan, more fun for the students, and more fun for you when you see the excitement of students learning music with joy and enthusiasm.

Busy teachers are always pressed for time to make careful plans for music instruction. Selecting songs or records sometimes takes all of the available time, leaving no opportunity for creating new ways to present and reinforce basic musical concepts. A dull, unbalanced music program can result. Adding an educational game to the music lesson can be the magical element that adds enthusiasm, and motivates productive learning by actively involving the student in each lesson. Such enthusiastic learning will inevitably improve teacher effectiveness.

Here is a collection of more than two hundred educational games for music classes which are specifically designed to improve teacher effectiveness and motivate student learning.

Some games are particularly recommended for one player. Others are suggested for small groups or large groups. This diversification makes the game collection useful for individualization or group instruction in both open-concept schools and traditionally structured classrooms.

The Table of Contents is, in reality, an annotated chart concisely listing each game, grade level, number of players,

4

equipment, and skill involved. This unique Table of Contents, organized by chapter titles, is designed to aid the diligent teacher in the search for a game involving a given musical skill or concept at a given grade level. Whether the teacher needs an Ear-Training Game for the primary grades, a Rhythm Game for the middle grades, or a Musical Literature Game for the junior high grades, he should be able to find it quickly and easily with the use of the Table of Contents.

The Appendix is devoted to offering complete instruction for making all of the equipment which is suggested for the games. The equipment has been kept simple and requires ordinary materials within most teachers' easy accessibility. In many cases the same equipment can be used for several games which adds to the worth of the teaching equipment. There are many games which require no special equipment at all.

The Index, at the end of the book, lists all game titles alphabetically and is another help to the busy teacher.

In thumbing through the book, the reader can see at the top of each page the basic concept which is reinforced by the games on that particular page. Then under each Game Title is listed the grade level, number of players, equipment, and complete directions for play.

Within the last decade, educators have become increasingly aware of the value of educational games for stimulating teaching techniques in all disciplines and at all grade levels. Some music teachers have for years recognized the value of games and have used game strategies in their teaching. Most, however, have not and consequently, many music classes have not kept abreast of new teaching techniques.

Here, in *A Galaxy of Games for the Music Class*, is an assemblage of original and adapted games which have been used successfully by experienced music teachers. Designed as a unique and complete collection, it should find a useful place in the library of every person who is concerned with the joy of teaching music.

CHAPTER I: GAMES FOR RHYTHMIC RESPONSE

CHAPTER II: GAMES FOR READING AND WRITING RHYTHM

CONTENTS

Title of Game	Grand Level	Number of Players
Floor Tic-Tac-Toe	K-2	Small or Large Group
Notes Up	K-3	Large Group
Rhythm Hats	K-8	Small Group
Rhythm Flash	K-8	Small or Large Group
Scrambled Song Rhythms	1-3	Small Group
Clap-A-Long	1-4	Individual, Small or Large Group
Rhythm Rondo	1-4	Large Group
Who's the Champ	1-8	Large Group
Which One Do You Hear?	1-8	Large Group
Around the Notes	2-3	Large Group
Rhythm Bee	2-8	Small or Large Group
Rhythm Bingo	2-8	Large Group
Rhythm Blocks: Large Group	2-8	Large Group
Rhythm Blocks: Small Group	2-8	Small Group
Toss-A-Cube	3-5	Small or Large Group
Building Beats	3-8	Small or Large Group
Building Measures	3-8	Small or Large Group
Musical Equations	3-8	Individual, Small or Large Group
Nix on Notes	3-8	Small or Large Group
Rhythm Special Flash	3-8	Small or Large Group
Flash and Add	4-8	Small or Large Group

Title of Game	Grade Level	Number of Players
Measure Up	4-8	Small Group
Musi-Matics	4-8	Individual, Small or Large Group
Chance Charts	5-8	Individual or Small Group
Four Square	5-8	Individual, Small or Large Group
How Many?	5-8	Individual, Small or Large Groups
Twenty One	5-8	Small Group
How Did I?	6-8	Large Group

CHAPTER III: GAMES FOR READING AND WRITING MELODY

Title of Game	Grade Level	Number of Players
Up, Down, or Same	K-3	Large or Small Groups
Which Tune is Different?	K-3	Small or Large Group
Which One Do You Hear?	1-8	Large Group
Read My Song	2-8	Small or Large Group
Scrambled Song Cards	2-8	Small Group
Guess the Rule	5-8	Small or Large Group
Melody Mix-Up	5-8	Individual or Small Group
Melody on Names	5-8	Individual or Small Group
Random Melody	5-8	Individual or Small Group

Title of Game	Grade Level	Number of Players
CHAPTER IV: GAMES FOR LEARNING MUSIC NOTATION		
Count Down	K-2	Large Group
Hokey-Pokey Notes	K-2	Large Group
Hop-O-My-Squares	K-2	Small or Large Group
I Spy	K-2	Large Group
Music Macrame	K-2	Individual, Small or Large Group
Musical Dominoes	K-2	Six or less
Note Matching	K-2	Individual
Taking a Line Walk	K-2	Small or Large Group
Taking a Space Walk	K-2	Small or Large Group
Touch and Find	K-2	Small or Large Group
Touch and Find: Team Game	K-2	Small or Large Group
Touch and Match	K-2	Individual
Touch and Point	K-2	Small or Large Group
Touch and Tell	K-2	Small or Large Group
Touch and Tell: Team Game	K-2	Small or Large Group
Which Card is Different?	K-2	Small or Large Group
Who Has the Card?	K-2	Large Group
Musical Fish	K-3	Small Group
Team Fishing	K-3	Small Group
Music Spy	K-8	Small or Large Group

Title of Game	Grade Level	Number of Players
Doghouse	1-3	Large Group
Ring Around the Alphabet	1-3	Large Group
Spin the Bottle	1-3	Small or Large Grcup
Staff-A-Live	1-3	Small or Large Group
Staff Hopscotch	1-3	Small or Large Group
Match My Card	2-3	Small Group
Naming Notes	2-3	Large Group
Notes Up the Staff	2-3	Large Group
Spaces of the Staff	2-4	Small or Large Group
What Am I?	2-4	Large Group
Bean Bags in the Lines	2-5	Large Group
Bean Bags in the Spaces	2-5	Large Group
Bean Bag Toss	2-5	Large Group
Camera	2-5	Large Group
Can You Find It?	2-5	Large Group
Find-The-Note-Relay	2-5	Small or Large Group
Intelligence Test	2-5	Small or Large Group
Music Hunt	2-5	Large Group
Musical Spell-It	2-5	Small or Large Group
Around the World	2-5	Small or Large Group
Name the Word	2-5	Small or Large Group
Grand Staff Bingo	2-8	Small or Large Group

14

Title of Game	Grade Level	Number of Players
Musical Speedway	2-8	Small or Large Group
Musical Stories	2-8	Individual, Small, or Large Group
Name-The-Note-Relay	2-8	Small or Large Group
Note Name Concentration	2-8	Small or Large Group
Treble Clef Bingo	2-8	Small or Large Group
Musical Spelling	3-5	Large Group
Wild Fish	3-5	Small Group
Bean Bag Toss	3-6	Small or Large Group
Music Twister	3-6	One at a time
Music Symbol Relay (Vocabulary)	3-8	Large Group
Secret Sentences	3-8	Small or Large Group
Music Symbol Concentration	4-8	Large Group
Making a Sound Composition	4-8	Small or Large Group
Newspaper Notes	4-8	Individual or Small Group
Pick-A-Pair	4-8	Three to six
Symbol-Match	4-8	Small Group
Team Treasure Hunt	4-8	Large Group
Three In a Row: Music Symbols	4-8	Large Group
Treasure Hunt	4-8	Large Group
Create a Story	5-8	Individual

19

CHAPTER VI: GAMES FOR DEVELOPING SINGING

Title of Game	Grade Level	Number of Players
CHAPTER VII: GAMES ABOUT COMPOSERS AND MUSIC LITER		
Tell the Theme	1-8	Small or Large Group
The Composer Bus	2-4	Small or Large Group
Composer Hunt	3-5	Small or Large Group
Composer Match	3-5	Four or less
Composer Match: Individual Game	3-5	Individual
Composer Match: Team Game	3-5	Large Group
On-The-Street Interviews	3-8	Small or Large Group
Whopper	3-8	Large Group
Composers in Rhythm	4-8	Large Group
Initial Who's Who	4-8	Large Group
Three in a Row: Composers	4-8	Large Group
Composer Clues	5-8	Individual or Small Group
Composer's Challenge	5-8	Large Group
Gotcha	5-8	Small or Large Group
Information Hunt	5-8	Small or Large Group
Interview a Composer	5-8	Small or Large Group
Scrambled Musicians	5-8	Small or Large Group
Symphony Hall	5-8	Two to Six
Top Hit Record Releases	5-8	Individual or Small Group

Title of Game	Grade Level	Number of Players
CHAPTER VIII: GAMES ABOUT MUSICAL INSTRUMENTS		
Special Instrument	K-2	Small or Large Group
Throw It Out	K-2	Small or Large Group
Which Instrument Is This?	K-2	Large Group
The Conductor Says	K-4	Large Group
Picture Puzzle	1-2	Individual
Blindfolded Panel	1-3	Large Group
See and Jump	1-3	Large Group
Fake Out	2-3	Large Group
Getting Closer	2-4	Two
What Instrument Is This?	2-4	Large Group
Which of the Families Do You Hear?	2-4	Large Group
Spin-An-Instrument	2-5	Small or Large Group
Draw An Instrument	2-5	Large Group
Classified Ads	3-5	Individual
Picture-Word Match	3-4	Individual, Small or Large Group
Choose a Match	3-5	Individual, Small or Large Group
Instrument Bingo	3-8	Large Group
Which Instrument Do You Hear?	3-8	Large Group
Who's the Conductor?	3-8	Large Group
Going to New York	4-8	Large Group

CHAPTER XI: MUSICAL WORD GAMES

APPENDIX: HOW TO MAKE

SUGGESTED GAME EQUIPMENT

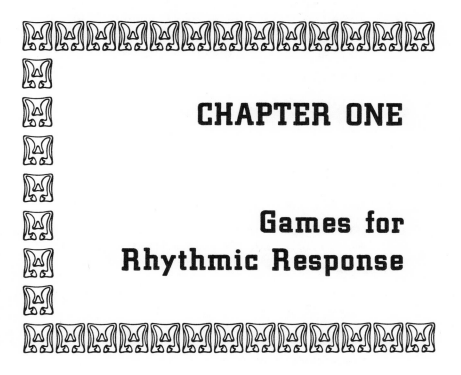

CHAPTER ONE

Games for
Rhythmic Response

ADD-A-CLAP

Grades: K-2

Number of Players: Large Group

Equipment: None

Directions:

The first player claps any pattern on a pre-determined number of beats (suggest 2 or 4). The second player immediately repeats that pattern and adds a pattern of his own (same length). The third

player repeats the patterns of each previous p.
adding one of his own. Play continues in this w.
until it becomes impossible! Then begin again s
that the entire class gets in on the fun!

Variation: Instead of clapping use stepping.

AS QUIET AS. . .

Grades: K-2

Number of Players: Large Group

Equipment: Several blank flash cards and marking pen,
or chalkboard and chalk. Recording of quiet music

Directions:

Students take turns naming the quietest thing they
can think of. As each thing is named, the teacher
writes it on a card. During the playing of the recording the teacher quietly calls the various cards and
the students quietly dramatize them.

HIDDEN ECHO CLAP

Grades: K-2

Number of Players: Small or Large Group

Equipment: None

Directions:

The teacher hides her hands behind the piano or a
screen while she claps a rhythm pattern. The players
must repeat what the teacher did.

REMEMBER THE BEAT

Grades: K-2

Number of Players: Small or Large Group

Equipment: Piano or recording

Directions:

The players walk or tap in rhythm as the music is played. The music is stopped and the rhythmic tapping should continue with an accurate beat. The music may begin or end at will, but the rhythmic tapping should be steadily heard.

SILENT ECHO CLAP

Grades: K-2

Number of Players: Small or Large Group

Equipment: None

Directions:

The teacher imitates the act of clapping a rhythm pattern, and the players must repeat what the teacher did.

WHAT DID I JUMP?

Grades: K-2

Number of Players: Large Group

Equipment: None

Directions:

> Player A is chosen to be "It." He jumps a rhythmic pattern and asks Player B to repeat the pattern. Player B then jumps the same pattern. A correct response earns the privilege of being "It."

COPYCAT

Grades: K-3

Number of Players: Large Group

Equipment: None

Directions:

> The teacher is the leader in making rhythmic motions that the class is asked to do along with him. The leader should change movements often enough to keep the game interesting, but not so often that it is confusing. To add interest, recorded music may be played to provide the pulse for the game. After a few days of this, the students will be able to take turns at being the leader. Suggested motions: snapping, clapping, leg-patting, tapping, touching shoulders, touching knees, opening and closing fingers, swaying, or putting one foot forward and back —whatever movements you think of are fine!

INSTRUMENTS AROUND THE ROOM

Grades: K-3

Number of Players: Large Group

Equipment: A rhythm instrument for each player. Piano or recording

Directions:

The chairs are arranged in a single circle. On each chair is a rhythm instrument. Each player stands behind the instrument of his choice. At a signal from the teacher, all of the players accompany the piano or recorded music. When the music stops, each player stops playing, moves to the next chair and prepares to play a new instrument. People who fail to stop or start on signal are eliminated from the game. If a teacher is a pianist, it works well to play three certain chords between instruments that always mean "Ready!" "Set!" "Play!" C, F and G₇ chords work fine!

Variation: If melody instruments are used, we recommend using the C pentatonic scale (c-d-e-g-a) and restricting your piano playing to the key of C.

ECHOES

Grades: K-8

Number of Players: Large Group

Equipment: None

Directions:

"Be my echo," the teacher says; and then he claps a four-beat pattern that the class repeats. The teacher answers with another four-beat pattern for the class to repeat; then another and so on. As the class gains skill they may move on to eight-beat patterns, or to using other body sounds such as tapping, clapping or leg-patting.
This one is a great waker-upper!

CIRCLE COUNTS

Grades: 1-3

Number of Players: Large Group

Equipment: Recording of march music

Directions:

> The students march around in a circle. The leader calls a number. The students then must form a circle containing that particular number. Players not included in the new circles are out. Remaining players march again.

Variation: Players not included in the new circle may form their own "left-over group" and thus not be eliminated.

SKITTLE, SKITTLE, SKITTLE, SKI

Grades: 1-8

Number of Players: Large Group

Equipment: None

Directions:

> The teacher says "Skittle, Skittle, Skittle, Ski. Do what I do after me." The class echoes the rhyme while the teacher goes on to a rhythmic motion for four beats. The class repeats those four beats while the teacher moves to another rhythmic motion for four beats, and another, creating a rhythmic canon between the teacher and the class. As the class gains skill at this, the rhythm patterns should become more complex. Suggested motions: snapping, clapping, leg-patting, tapping.

TULIPS IN 3/4 TIME

Grades: 2-3

Number of Players: Large Group

Equipment: Paper and pencil for each player. Recording (or piano) to provide music in a slow 3/4 time

Directions:

While listening to the music each player draws tulips like this: A downward stroke on beat one and two short strokes for leaves on beats two and three. The petals are made by a curved stroke on beat one and the two final petal strokes on beats two and three.

WHO STOLE THE CANDY?

Grades: 3-5

Number of Players: Large Group

Equipment: None

Directions:

The class chants the following rhyme while keeping a steady rhythmic accompaniment: clap, snap, clap, snap.

Class: "Who stole the candy from the superstore? Who stole the candy from the superstore?"

Solo: "__John__ stole the candy from the super-store."

Class: "__John__ stole the candy from the super-
store."
John: "Who me?"
Class: "Yes you!"
John: "Couldn't be!"
Class: "Then Who?"

Repeat the chant beginning with line three and naming a new person. The game continues with each of
the accused naming a new suspect.

RHYTHM PUZZLE

Grades: 3-8

Number of Players: Large Group

Equipment: None

Directions:

"It" stands in front of the class and claps the rhythm
of a familiar song. He calls on other players to name
the song that he is clapping. The player who names
the song correctly gets to be "It" for the next round.

AGENT FROM TEMPO

Grades: 4-8

Number of Players: Small or Large Group

Equipment: None

Directions:

The first player claps a rhythm pattern for a designated number of beats. The second player repeats
that pattern *at the same tempo*, and adds a pattern
of his own. The play continues around the group

maintaining the tempo and stopping only when the play becomes impossible.

RHYTHM GAME

Grades: 4-8

Number of Players: Large Group

Equipment: None

Directions:

> A continuous rhythmic pattern (leg-pat, clap, leg-pat, clap) accompanies the group chant. Once the pattern is well established the chant begins.
>
> Group chants: "Rhythm, rhythm, that's our game; You play a pattern; we'll play the same."
>
> Solo rhythm pattern: Eight beats duration, group rests.
>
> Group repeats the solo: Repeat from the beginning with a new soloist.

RHYTHM

Grades: 5-8

Number of Players: Large Group

Equipment: None

Directions:

> The chairs are numbered in order—one for each player. The class must keep a steady beat with the following motions: patting the legs twice, clapping the hands twice, and snapping the fingers twice. The

pattern, then, is like this: pat, pat, clap, clap, snap, snap. When any player's number is called, he must respond by speaking his own number on the first snap and any other number on the second snap —and he must respond in rhythm. When a player misses he must move to the last chair and everybody between him and the last chair may move closer to the number one. The object of the game is to move up to the number one chair.

AUGMENTATION

Grades: 6-8

Number of Players: Large Group

Equipment: None

Directions:

Each player echo-claps a rhythm given by the teacher; and then claps it again in augmented rhythm.

Variation: Put the augmented pattern into the feet.

DIMINUTION

Grades: 6-8

Number of Players: Large Group

Equipment: None

Directions:

The student echo-claps a rhythm, and then puts the diminution of the rhythm into his feet or a body sound.

Variation: Try this with the eyes closed.

RETROGRADE

Grades: 6-8

Number of Players: Large Group

Equipment: Chalkboard and chalk or prepared chart

Directions:

The students read a series of displayed rhythms—first forward, then backward.

Variation: Students echo-clap a simple rhythm given by the teacher—first forward, then backward.

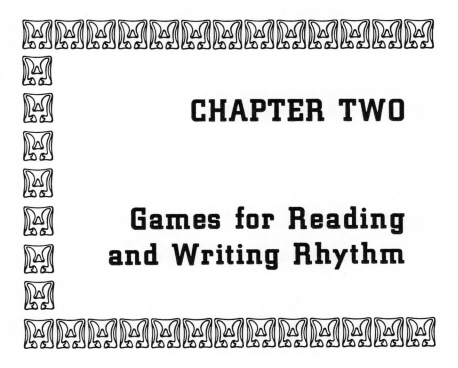

CHAPTER TWO

Games for Reading and Writing Rhythm

THROW IT OUT

Grades: K-2

Number of Players: Small or Large Group

Equipment: Deck of Note-Value Cards (See Appendix)

Directions:

The players are divided into two teams. The contestant is shown a set of four cards—three alike and one different. He eliminates the one that does not belong. A correct response earns a team point.

NOTES-UP

Grades: K-3

Number of Players: Large Group

Equipment: Note-Value Cards (See Appendix)

Directions:

This game is patterned after the well known "Seven-Up." Seven students are chosen to be "It." They are each given a different Note-Value Card. The other players put their heads down on their desks or close their eyes. The seven "Its" quietly place their cards in the hands of seven other students. The new card-holders now, one by one, identify the card which they hold and guess which "It" gave it to him. Play is continued with the new card-holders being "Its."

RHYTHM HATS

Grades: K-8

Number of Players: Small Group

Equipment: Rhythm Cards (See Appendix). Assorted collection of hats

Directions:

A different Rhythm Card is given to each player. The teacher claps and/or chants one of the rhythm patterns. The player who is holding that particular card raises his hand. If his is a correct response, he gets to choose a hat to wear for the duration of the game or as designated by the teacher.

RHYTHM FLASH

Grades: K-8

Number of Players: Small or Large Group

Equipment: Rhythm Cards (See Appendix)

Directions:

The teacher challenges the class to clap and/or chant the rhythm patterns on all the cards at a continuous tempo. The teacher flashes the cards quickly to see if the class can perform with no mistakes.

Variations: Try flashing the cards with increasing speed so that the cards are eventually one or two complete patterns ahead of the one being performed. This is a real challenge!

FLOOR TIC-TAC-TOE

Grades: K-2

Number of Players: Small or Large Group

Equipment: Nine Rhythm Cards (See Appendix). Five sheets red paper 12″ x 18″. Five sheets yellow paper 12″ x 18″

Directions:

The Rhythm Cards are placed on the floor in three rows with three cards in each row. The players are divided into two teams. The first player chooses a Rhythm Card, points to his choice, and claps or chants it in rhythm. If his performance is correct, he covers the card with a sheet of red paper which represents his team. The play passes to a member of the opposite team who uses the yellow paper to cover correct answers. The team that is first to cover a row of three (vertically, horizontally, or diagonally) is the winner of the game.

SCRAMBLED SONG RHYTHMS

Grades: 1-3

Number of Players: Small Group

Equipment: Several sets of prepared Rhythm Pattern Cards. (Each set should consist of the rhythm for a complete song with a phrase appearing on each card. Choose simple, familiar songs like: "Hot Cross Buns," "Jingle Bells," "Clap, Clap, Clap Your Hands.")

Directions:

Each group is handed a set of cards and given the title of the song to which those cards belong. The team then has two jobs: To arrange the cards in the proper order and to clap the complete song as it appears on the cards.

CLAP A-LONG

Grades: 1-4

Number of Players: Individual, Small or Large Group

Equipment: Rhythm Cards (See Appendix). Recorded music (slow 4/4)

Directions:

Show a card as the music is played. The players clap the pattern in rhythm to the music, changing patterns as the teacher displays different cards.

RHYTHM RONDO

Grades: 1-4

Number of Players: Large Group

Equipment: Rhythm Cards (See Appendix)

Directions:

> The group selects one of the Rhythm Cards to be the recurring "A" Theme. After firmly establishing this pattern, by clapping and/or chanting, the play begins. The group begins by clapping and/or chanting the established A Theme and repeating it after each new card is shown. In this way a Rhythm Rondo is created: A-B-A-C-A-D-A. This game may continue for several minutes, varying the A Theme each time.

WHO'S THE CHAMP?

Grades: 1-8

Number of Players: Large Group

Equipment: 6 Magic Slates

Directions:

> Six contestants are seated in front of the class. Their job is to write a rhythm pattern as it is dictated by the teacher. Those who miss are replaced by new players—until finally only the "champ" remains.

WHICH ONE DO YOU HEAR?

Grades: 1-8

Number of Players: Large Group

Equipment: Three different rhythm patterns written on chalkboard or chart

Directions:

"It" claps one of the patterns. A selected student should identify the one that was clapped. A correct response earns the privilege of being "It" in the next round. The difficulty of the rhythm patterns can be varied endlessly to make this game appropriately difficult for any level.

Variation 1: "It" may use a drum instead of a clap.

Variation 2: "It" may use any instrument of his choice.

Variation 3: The class may be divided into teams with the teams alternating the problems. Each correct response earns a team point.

AROUND THE NOTES

Grades: 2-3

Number of Players: Large Group

Equipment: Note-Value Cards (See Appendix). Piano or recorded music

Directions:

The Note-Value Cards are placed in a circle on the floor. "It" stands in the center of the circle. The other children stand behind the cards. Start the music and the children walk around the circle. When the music stops, "It" points to one of the players and he has to name the note or rest that he stopped behind. Success means that he is the new "It."

RHYTHM BEE

Grades: 2-8

Number of Players: Small or Large Group

Equipment: Rhythm Cards (See Appendix)

Directions:

This is patterned after an old-fashioned Spelling Bee. Players stand in a line. The teacher shows a card to each player in turn, who is supposed to clap and/or chant the pattern. If he misses, he must be seated; but if he gives a correct response he remains standing. The person who remains standing for the longest is the winner.

RHYTHM BINGO

Grades: 2-8

Number of Players: Large Group

Equipment: A Bingo Grid prepared on a transparency for use on the overhead projector (or it may be written on the chalkboard). 24 pieces of paper to use with the transparency—12 circles and 12 squares. 2 pieces of colored chalk if you use chalkboard

Directions:

The players are divided into two teams. The grid is displayed to everyone. Taking turns, each student choses his own problem; then he performs it by clapping or playing the drum. If he is correct, that spot is covered with his team's symbol (circle, square, or colored chalk). A straight line of team symbols means victory for that team!

	B	**I**	**N**	**G**	**O**
1	I ⊓	I ⌐I	⊓⌐	⌐I⊓	⊓ I I
2	⊓I⊓	⊓⌐⊓	⊓⊓	I ⌐	I I I
3	I ⌐⊓	I I ⊓	⊓I⌐	I ⊓	I I
4	I I ⌐	⊓⌐I	I⊓I	⊓I ♪	⊓I I
5	⊓⊓⊓	I⊓I	⊓I⌐	I ⌐ ⌐	⊓I

Variation: Prepare several grids of varying difficulty.

RHYTHM BLOCKS: LARGE GROUP

Grades: 2-8

Number of Players: Large Group

Equipment: Rhythm Blocks (See Appendix)

Directions:

Players are divided into two teams. Each team has a set of Rhythm Blocks for its use. It is explained that the blocks are used to represent certain note values. The eighth note, quarter note, half note, and whole notes are represented by the smallest to the largest blocks, respectively. A player from each team participates in each round. The contestants take their places near their set of Rhythm Blocks. The teacher claps or chants a rhythm pattern, and the contestants work to notate it with the blocks. The contestant who is first to correctly complete the task is the winner and he earns a point for his team. The play passes to new contestants in each new round. The team with the most points at the end of play is the winner. Be sure to give patterns that use only the note values that the players have.

RHYTHM BLOCKS: SMALL GROUPS

Grades: 2-8

Number of Players: Small Group

Equipment: Rhythm Blocks (See Appendix)

Directions:

Each player has a partner and each couple is given a set of Rhythm Blocks. It is explained that the blocks are used to represent certain note-values. The eighth note, quarter note, half note, and whole notes are represented by the smallest to the largest blocks, respectively. When the teacher claps or chants a rhythm pattern, each couple works to notate it with the blocks. The couple who is first to complete the task correctly is the winner. Be sure to give patterns that use only the note-values that the players have.

Variation: Combine two sets of Rhythm Blocks and dictate longer patterns.

TOSS-A-CUBE

Grades: 3-5

Number of Players: Small or Large Group

Equipment: Toss-A-Cube (See Appendix). A tabletop for

the playing area. Chalkboard and chalk for a score board

Directions:

Players are divided into two teams. One player at a time, from alternating teams, tosses the cube on the table. The score is posted after each toss according to the following: quarter note = 1; half note = 2; dotted half note = 3; whole note = 4; quarter rest = miss one turn; half rest = miss two turns. The highest score determines the winner.

BUILDING BEATS

Grades: 3-8

Number of Players: Small or Large Group

Equipment: Rhythm Blocks (See Appendix)

Directions:

Players are divided into two teams. Each team is given two sets of Rhythm Blocks for its use. It is explained that the blocks are used to represent certain note values. The eighth note, quarter note, half note, and whole notes are represented by the smallest to the largest blocks, respectively. A player from each team participates in each round. The contestants take their places near their set of Rhythm Blocks. The teacher calls a number one through eight. Upon that signal, the contestants attempt to notate with the blocks the exact number of beats that the teacher has called. The player who is first to complete the task correctly is the winner and he earns a point for his team. The team with the most points at the end of play is the winner.

Variation: The teacher may impose certain restrictions on the contestants such as: "Construct four beats without using a whole note"; "Construct two beats without using a half note" or "Construct seven beats without using a whole note."

BUILDING MEASURES

Grades: 3-8

Number of Players: Small or Large Group

Equipment: Note-Value Cards (See Appendix)

Directions:

The players are divided into two teams. The Note-Value Cards are shuffled and stacked, face down. The teacher calls any number one through eight. The object of the game is for the players to turn up the cards, building a measure until they have the exact number of beats called for. A player from Team A turns up the first card and places it on the display rack. (The tray of the chalkboard is great for this; a stack of books might also work.) A player from Team B then turns up the second card and places it beside the first card. Play continues in this way until the exact number desired is attained. The team that makes the completing play earns a point. If the card turned up should be of greater value than is needed, that card is discarded and play continues until the exact card turns up. The cards are re-shuffled for each new round. The team that has the most points at the end of play is the winner.

MUSICAL EQUATIONS

Grades: 3-8

Number of Players: Individual, Small or Large Group

Equipment: Chalkboard, chalk

Directions:

The players are divided into two teams. The teacher writes an equation on the board. Team A attempts to complete the equation verbally. A time limit is imposed. Team B then has a turn. Complexity of problems is determined by ability level of the class.

Variation: For individuals, use written answers.

$$\textrm{\musNote{half}} + \underline{\hspace{1.5em}} = \textrm{\musNote{whole}}$$

$$\textrm{\musNote{dotted half}} + \underline{\hspace{1.5em}} = \textrm{\musNote{whole}}$$

$$\underline{\hspace{1.5em}} + \textrm{\musNote{two eighths}} = \textrm{\musNote{half}}$$

$$\textrm{\musNote{whole}} - \underline{\hspace{1.5em}} = \textrm{\musNote{half}}$$

$$\textrm{\musNote{half}} - \underline{\hspace{1.5em}} = \textrm{\musNote{quarter}}$$

$$\textrm{\musNote{quarter}} + \underline{\hspace{1.5em}} = \textrm{\musNote{half}}$$

$$\textrm{\musNote{two eighths}} + \underline{\hspace{1.5em}} = \textrm{\musNote{half}}$$

$$\textrm{\musNote{eighth triplet}} + \underline{\hspace{1.5em}} = \textrm{\musNote{quarter}}$$

$$\textrm{\musNote{half}} + \underline{\hspace{1.5em}} = \textrm{\musNote{dotted half}}$$

$$\textrm{\musNote{eighth rest}} + \underline{\hspace{1.5em}} = \textrm{\musNote{quarter rest}}$$

$$\textrm{\musNote{quarter rest}} - \textrm{\musNote{eighth rest}} = \underline{\hspace{1.5em}}$$

NIX ON NOTES

Grades: 3-8

Number of Players: Small or Large Group

Equipment: Prepared sheet for each player or large chart

Directions:

Cross out the measures that do not contain exactly three counts. Chant the rhythm of the remaining measures (Sing "Eidelweiss" to it).

RHYTHM SPECIAL-FLASH

Grades: 3-8

Number of Players: Small or Large Group

Equipment: Rhythm Cards (See Appendix)

Directions:

> Someone chooses one card that will be the "Special-Flash" Card. The group memorizes the pattern on that particular card; then returns the card to the stack. The teacher flashes the cards before the class so that they can clap and/or chant each rhythm pattern. When the "Special-Flash" card turns up, the players should stand while they clap or chant the pattern. This is a good way to incorporate a little "change of position" into a group that has been sitting for a while!

FLASH AND ADD

Grades: 4-8

Number of Players: Small or Large Group

Equipment: Note-Value Cards (See Appendix)

Directions:

> Note-Value Cards are shuffled and flashed one by one. Players add the note values aloud in cumulative addition. This is a good mathematical drill!

Variation: Make the game a little harder by using Note-Value Playing Cards instead of Note-Value Cards. When you do this, use your finger to cover the figure in the corner of each card. Using the Note-Value Playing Cards works better with small groups than large groups because the cards are small.

MEASURE UP

Grades: 4-8

Number of Players: 3 or 4

Equipment: Deck of Note-Value Cards (See Appendix). Time Signature Spinner (See Appendix)

Directions:

Each player is dealt five Note-Value Cards. The remaining Note-Value Cards are stacked in the center. Each player then spins to determine what his time signature will be for this game. The object of the game is to acquire cards that make complete measures (sets) in the respective time signature which the player has determined. The first player draws a card from the stack and discards if he chooses. Play continues. As sets are collected they are laid out. The player who collects the most sets is the winner.

MUSI-MATICS

Grades: 4-8

Number of Players: Individual, Small or Large Group

Equipment: Chalkboard, chalk

Directions:

Put one of these on the chalkboard for some mental gymnastics.

1.	♩♩♩	is to	♩.	as	♫ is to	_____
2.	♩	is to	o	as	_____ is to	♩.
3.	♪	is to	♩	as	♩ is to	_____
4.	o	is to	♩	as	♩ is to	_____
5.	❙	is to	♪	as	_____ is to	♩
6.	♬	is to	♩	as	_____ is to	♩
7.	▬	is to	♩	as	❙ is to	_____
8.	♫	is to	♩	as	♩♩ is to	_____
9.	♩	is to	♩	as	♪ is to	_____
10.	❙	is to	▬	as	▬ is to	_____

CHANCE CHANTS

Grades: 5-8

Number of Players: Individual or Small Group

Equipment: A descriptive picture for each player or group

Directions:

The student is given a picture. His task is to create a simple verse to describe the picture. He should write the rhythm pattern above each line of his verse.

Variation: The student is given a verse and must create the rhythm pattern for it.

FOUR SQUARE

Grades: 5-8

Number of Players: Individual, Small or Large Group

Equipment: Chalkboard and chalk. Paper and pencil for each player

Directions:

Each student draws a grid on his paper similar to the one illustrated. His job is to make different combinations of notes that add up to the numbers at the left of the grid (horizontally) and, also, must add up to numbers at the top of the grid (vertically). This is a challenging mental exercise! It is suggested that a list of notes be drawn on the chalkboard from which the player might choose.

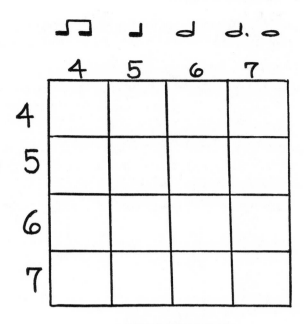

HOW MANY?

Grades: 5-8

Number of Players: Individual, Small or Large Group

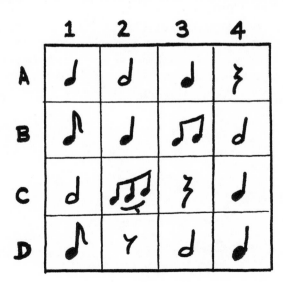

Equipment: Prepared game sheet for each player (or the work may be written on the chalkboard or a chart)

Directions:

The teacher asks "How many lines contain notes that will equal a measure in 4/4 time when added together?"

Variation: Create a more complex board and ask, "Find some random squares that equal the number of beats in a measure of 4/4 time."

Variation: Add total note values horizontally or vertically.

TWENTY ONE

Grades: 5-8

Number of Players: Small Group

Equipment: A Deck of Note-Value Cards (See Appendix)

Directions:

Two cards are given to each player. Remaining cards are placed in a stack. Each player then takes his turn by requesting a specific note or rest from any other player. If that player can't help, the first player draws from the stack, and play continues. The first player to reach exactly 21 counts is the winner.

HOW DID I?

Grades: 6-8

Number of Players: Large Group

Equipment: Chalkboard, chalk

Directions:

The teacher writes on the chalkboard a pattern similar to set "A." The students compete to determine the pattern used by the teacher in set "A." Then, using that same pattern, they complete set "B."

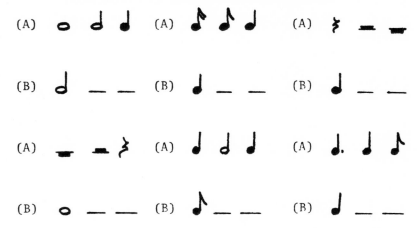

This is a dandy for that extra minute left at the end of the lesson!

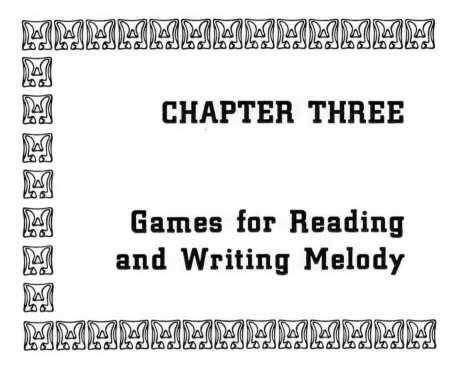

CHAPTER THREE

Games for Reading and Writing Melody

UP, DOWN, OR SAME

Grades: K-3

Number of Players: Small or Large Group

Equipment: Melody Cards (See Appendix)

Directions:

Players are divided into two teams. Three Melody Cards are displayed. Each player, in turn, is asked to tell which of the three cards shows a melody that is moving up? Down? Repeating the same tones? A correct answer earns a point for the team. The team with the most points is the winner. The teacher should change and rearrange the cards at will.

WHICH TUNE IS DIFFERENT?

Grades: K-3

Number of Players: Small or Large Group

Equipment: Two sets of Melody Cards (See Appendix)

Directions:

Three Melody Cards are displayed. Two should be alike and one should be different. The player is asked to select the one that is different. A correct response might earn a paper badge that says "Good Music Reader" to be taped to the dress or shirt.

WHICH ONE DO YOU HEAR?

Grades: 1-8

Number of Players: Large Group

Equipment: Melody Cards (See Appendix)

Directions:

Players are divided into two teams. Three Melody Cards are displayed. The teacher plays or sings one of the displayed patterns. A selected student should identify the one that was sung. A correct response earns a team point. The difficulty of the melodic patterns can be varied endlessly to make this game appropriately difficult for any level.

READ MY SONG

Grades: 2-8

Number of Players: Small or Large Group

Equipment: None

Directions:

"It" stands in front of the group with a familiar tune in his mind. He makes no sound and uses his hand in the air to show the melody direction of his tune. The player who correctly figures out his tune gets to be "It" in the next round.

SCRAMBLED SONG CARDS

Grades: 2-8

Number of Players: Small Group

Equipment: Several sets of Song Cards (See Appendix)

Directions:

Players should be divided into groups of four. Each group is handed a set of scrambled Song Cards and is given the title of the song to which those cards belong. The group then has two jobs: (1) to arrange the cards in the proper order and (2) to sing the complete song as it appears on the cards.

GUESS THE RULE

Grades: 5-8

Number of Players: Small or Large Group

Equipment: Several prepared charts or transparencies, each prepared with four phrases on them. (On each chart or transparency the four phrases should have a common factor such as time signature, key signature, or any element of notation.)

Directions:

Each player, in turn, is shown a set of four musical phrases. His job is to "Guess the Rule" of construction. In other words, what do these four phrases have in common? The common factor may be any element of notation.

MELODY MIX-UP

Grades: 5-8

Number of Players: Individual or Small Group

Equipment: 11″ x 18″ sheet prepared with staff, clef sign, key signature, time signature, and bar lines for each individual or group. An envelope containing music symbols that are proportionate to the size of the staff for each individual or group. Suggested symbols:

Directions:

The assignment is to construct a melody using only the contents of the envelope.

Variation 1: Using the same envelope contents, construct a melody with no pre-determined key or meter. Each group may choose its own.

Variation 2: Again with no pre-determined key or meter,

shake the envelope contents onto the staff. Rearrange only if necessary, thus creating some chance music.

MELODY ON NAMES

Grades: 5-8

Number of Players: Individual or Small Group

Equipment: Resonator Bells. Chalkboard

Directions:

Write the name of a student or any famous person on the chalkboard. Circle the letters found in the musical alphabet. Select a bell to correspond with each of the circled letters. Create a melody using only these bells. Notate the melody on music manuscript.

RANDOM MELODY

Grades: 5-8

Number of Players: Individual or Small Group

Equipment: Resonator Bells. Bits of paper containing one note-name (A, B, B, C, C#, etc.)

Directions:

Each student or group draws four note-names from a box. Select resonator bells that correspond to the note-names. Create a melody using only these bells. Notate the melody on music manuscript.

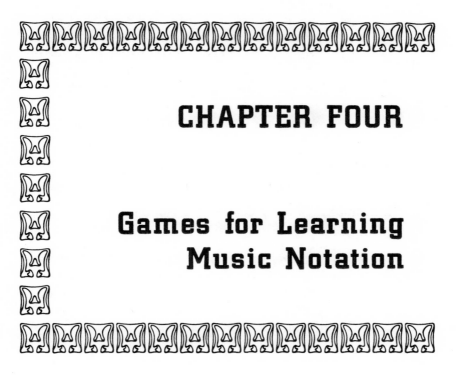

CHAPTER FOUR

Games for Learning Music Notation

COUNT DOWN

Grades: K-2

Number of Players: Large Group

Equipment: Primary Cards (See Appendix)

Directions:

Players are organized into two teams. Two sets of the Primary Cards are placed in random order on the floor or chalk tray, with each set being placed in a different part of the room. The teams line up near their respective set of cards. The teacher calls a music symbol from one of the cards. The first player on each team races to see who can be first to pick up the correct card and earn a point for his team. The team that earns the most points is the winner.

HOKEY-POKEY NOTES

Grades: K-2

Number of Players: Large Group

Equipment: Primary Cards (See Appendix)

Directions:

Players are standing in a circle with each player holding a card. The appropriate cards are put "in" and "out" as the following words are sung to the tune "Hokey Pokey."

"You put your whole note in;
 You put your whole note out;
 You put your whole note in;
 And you shake it all about."
(Everybody move:)
 "You do the Hokey Pokey and you
 Turn yourself about;
 That's what it's all about!"
Repeat the game naming different symbols each time.

HOP-O-MY-SQUARES

Grades: K-2

Number of Players: Small or Large Group

Equipment: Vinyl Floor Chart (See Appendix). (Cover the bottom half.)

Directions:

Players are organized into two teams. One player from each team competes in a round. The teacher draws a symbol on the board that matches one on the Vinyl Chart. The player hops to the symbol matching the one drawn. A point is given for each correct move. The team with the most points is the winner.

Variation No. 1: The player hops onto the square that the teacher calls.

Variation No. 2: The teacher writes three symbols on the board; the students hop the pattern.

Variation No. 3: The teacher writes a pattern of three symbols; then quickly erases them. The student must hop the pattern from memory.

I SPY

Grades: K-2

Number of Players: Large Group

Equipment: Existing bulletin board displays

Directions:

The teacher, looking around the room, says "I spy a music symbol that means to rest for one beat." The player who can correctly find the designated symbol is the winner for that round.

MUSIC MACRAMÉ

Grades: K-2

Number of Players: Individual Small or Large Group

Equipment: Music Macramé Cards (See Appendix). A length of yarn for each player (about 20")

Directions:

> The teacher names a music symbol. The player inserts his yarn in the hole beside the symbol. The teacher calls another symbol, and the player stretches the thread over to the hole nearest that particular symbol. As the game progresses, with the teacher naming the various symbols that appear on the card, a design is formed on the card. Since all the cards are the same, a student may check his work by noticing if his design is the same as other players. At the end of play, all designs should be the same.

Variation 1: Call the symbols in a different order to create a different design.

Variation 2: Have students take turns being the leader so that they can have the experience of naming the various music symbols that appear on the cards.

MUSICAL DOMINOES

Grades: K-2

Number of Players: Six or less

Equipment: Musical Domino Cards (See Appendix)

Directions:

> Shuffle the Domino Cards and deal six cards to each

player. Place remaining cards to one side in the "Boneyard." The first player begins by placing any card face up on the table. The player to his left places a card with a matching picture beside the first card. Play continues around the table with each player matching an exposed card that has been played previously. When a player cannot play a matching card from his own hand, he may draw one card from the Boneyard although he may not discard during that turn. The player who is first to use all of his cards is the winner.

NOTE MATCHING

Grades: K-2

Number of Players: Individual

Equipment: Two sets of Treble Clef Note Cards (See Appendix)

Directions:

The two sets of cards are shuffled together. The player spreads out all the cards and then finds each pair that matches.

TAKING A LINE WALK

Grades: K-2

Number of Players: Small or Large Group

Equipment: Floor Staff (See Appendix)

Directions:

Two students compete in each round. Their task is to walk horizontally along a line of the Staff without getting off that line. One miss and the player is out.

TAKING A SPACE WALK

Grades: K-2

Number of Players: Small or Large Group

Equipment: Floor Staff (See Appendix)

Directions:

> Two students compete in each round. Their task is to walk horizontally along a certain space of the Staff without touching a line. One miss and the player is out.

TOUCH AND FIND

Grades: K-2

Number of Players: Small or Large Group

Equipment: Tactile Cards (See Appendix)

Directions:

> "It" stands before the group with his eyes closed. The leader places three Tactile Cards before him and says, naming one of the three cards, "Find the quarter note." "It" feels all three cards, and then selects the one that is requested and presents it to the leader. A new "It" is selected as play continues.

TOUCH AND FIND: TEAM GAME

Grades: K-2

Number of Players: Small or Large Group

Equipment: Tactile Cards (See Appendix)

Directions:

Players are divided into two teams. A player from each team competes in each round. The contestants come before the group and close their eyes (or you may use blindfolds). The teacher places three identical Tactile Cards before the contestants and asks them to select the "quarter note card" (or whatever you have used). The contestant who is first to find the requested card is the winner of that round and earns a point for his team. Play continues with two new contestants and different cards. At the end of play, the team that has the most points is the winner.

TOUCH AND MATCH

Grades: K-2

Number of Players: Individual

Equipment: Two sets of Tactile Cards (See Appendix)

Directions:

The two sets of Tactile Cards are shuffled together. The player must close his eyes or wear a blindfold. He spreads out all the cards and then finds each pair that matches.

TOUCH AND POINT

Grades: K-2

Number of Players: Small or Large Group

Equipment: Tactile Cards (See Appendix)

Directions:

"It" stands before the group with his eyes closed.

One Tactile Card is placed before him for him to feel. He feels it and takes his hands away from the card, opens his eyes, and is shown three Tactile Cards that include the one he felt. His job is to point to the one he felt. Another "It" is chosen as the play continues.

TOUCH AND TELL

Grades: K-2

Number of Players: Small or Large Group

Equipment: Tactile Cards (See Appendix)

Directions:

"It" stands before the group with his eyes closed. One Tactile Card is placed before him. With his eyes closed, he feels the card; and, with his eyes still closed, he names the symbol that he felt. A new "It" is selected as play continues.

TOUCH AND TELL—TEAM GAME

Grades: K-2

Number of Players: Small or Large Group

Equipment: Two sets of Tactile Cards (See Appendix)

Directions:

Players are divided into two teams. A player from each team competes in each round. The contestants come before the group and close their eyes. The teacher hands the two contestants identical Tactile

Cards. With their eyes closed, the contestants feel the cards and name the music symbol that appears there. The student who is first to accomplish the task earns a point for his team. Play continues with a new pair of contestants. The team that has the most points at the end of play is the winner.

WHICH CARD IS DIFFERENT?

Grades: K-2

Number of Players: Small or Large Group

Equipment: Primary Cards (See Appendix)

Directions:

The teacher displays three cards in front of the group. Two cards should match; one should be different. The teacher calls one player by name and says: "_____, find the card that's different before I count to five. One, two, three, four, five." When the chosen student has accomplished his task, three new cards are displayed, and the play continues.

Variation: Play this game using Treble Clef Note Cards. (See Appendix.)

WHO HAS THE CARD?

Grades: K-2

Number of Players: Large Group

Equipment: Primary Cards (See Appendix)

Directions:

Each player closes his eyes and is given a Primary Card. The teacher ("It") says, "Card, Card, Who has the Quarter Note Card?" (or some other symbol). The players with the appropriate cards stand and are the winners. Players may take turns at being "It." After a few rounds, cards may be traded to enhance interest.

MUSICAL FISH

Grades: K-3

Number of Players: Small Group

Equipment: Magnetic Fish and Fishing Pole (See Appendix). Fishbowl or box

Directions:

Each player is given an opportunity to use the pole and fish from the bowl. The player then identifies the symbol that he catches and he may keep it. If he is unable to identify it, he must "throw it back." At the end of the game, the player with the most fish is the winner.

TEAM FISHING

Grades: K-3

Number of Players: Small Group

Equipment: Magnetic Fish (See Appendix). Magnetic Board

Directions:

Players are divided into two teams. The fish are spread out (face up) on a table. The first player names a symbol, picks it up and places it on his team's side of the board. The second player, from the opposite team, selects another fish, names it, and places it on the magnetic board. Play continues until all the fish are gone or the players can name no more. The team with the most fish is the winner.

Variation: Play the game with the fish face down. This is a little harder.

MUSIC SPY

Grades: K-8

Number of Players: Small or Large Group

Equipment: Chalkboard and chalk

Directions:

A group of music symbols and different kinds of notes are drawn on the chalkboard. The players take a few seconds to name each symbol and get it in their memory. Then the players close their eyes and one or more symbols is erased. The players open their eyes and guess what was erased. As the game continues, additional symbols are erased, and the students are always required to name the most recent deletions as well as all previous ones. Students love this kind of memory drill!

Variation: Draw the music symbols in straight rows from left to right. Have the players recite the list of symbols from left to right. As symbols are erased during the memory drill, have them continue to name the list in order, naming both the ones that appear as well as those that have been erased.

DOGHOUSE

Grades: 1-3

Number of Players: Large Group

Equipment: A Cardboard Doghouse. Musical Symbol Flashcards (See Appendix)

Directions:

The students will name each card as it is shown by the teacher. Any cards that are missed will be put into the Doghouse for further drill. This is great fun for a warm-up drill!

RING AROUND THE ALPHABET

Grades: 1-3

Number of Players: Large Group

Equipment: Treble Clef Note Cards (See Appendix). Recording or piano music

Directions:

Place Treble Clef Note Cards in a circle on the floor. A student stands behind each card. Students walk around the circle as the music is played. When the music stops, the students stop behind a card. The teacher calls the name of a specific note. The child who has that note raises his card. Play continues.

Variation: When the music stops, each child takes turns naming his note.

SPIN THE BOTTLE

Grades: 1-3

Number of Players: Small or Large Group

Equipment: Primary or Music Symbol Cards

Directions:

> The players are divided into two teams. They stand in a single circle with players from Team A and Team B alternating around the circle. Each player is given a Music Symbol Card that is laid on the floor in front of him. The bottle is placed on its side in the center of the circle. "It" spins the bottle. When the bottle stops spinning "It" must name the symbol on the card toward which the bottle is pointing. A correct answer earns a point for his team. Play continues around the circle with the winner being the team that has the most points.

STAFF A-LIVE

Grades: 1-3

Number of Players: Small or Large Group

Equipment: Floor Staff (See Appendix)

Directions:

> Using the Floor Staff, a student puts his feet on the bottom line, his knee on the second line, his waist on the third line, his shoulders on the fourth line, and his head on the fifth line. The teacher may change directions to further complicate the task.

STAFF HOPSCOTCH

Grades: 1-3

Number of Players: Small or Large Group

Equipment: Floor Staff (See Appendix)

Directions:

Three or four students compete in each round. Their task is to hop on one foot vertically across the Staff touching only the lines—or hop only on the spaces. The teacher calls for "lines" or "spaces." One miss and the player is "out."

MATCH MY CARD

Grades: 2-3

Number of Players: Small Group

Equipment: Primary Cards (See Appendix)

Directions:

Cards are displayed at the front of the room. Two teams of four players each stand on either side of the cards. A player from Team A points to a card. A player from Team B must name the symbol and draw one on the chalkboard. One point is given for correctly naming the symbol; another point is given for correctly writing it. The team with the most points at the end of play is the winner.

NAMING NOTES

Grades: 2-3

Number of Players: Large Group

Equipment: Treble Clef Note Cards (See Appendix)

Directions:

A card is given to every player. The first player displays his card, names the note, and leaves the card on the display rack. (The tray of the chalkboard is great for this; a stack of books might also work.) Each succeeding player must name all previously named notes and then his own.

Variation: This could be a team game by having two teams and using one player at a time from alternate teams. Correct answers, in this variation, would earn a point for the team.

NOTES UP THE STAFF

Grades: 2-4

Number of Players: Large Group

Equipment: Chalkboard with two music staves. Chalk

Directions:

The class should be divided into two teams for this relay game. The object is for each team to write notes diatonically up and down the staff without missing a single line or space. The first person on each team writes a note on the first line; the second person writes a note on the first space; the third person makes his note on the second line etc. The team to write the pattern first correctly is the winner.

SPACES ON THE STAFF

Grades: 2-4

Number of Players: Small or Large Group

Equipment: One or two music flannel boards and flannel notes or discs

Directions:

The class is divided into two teams. One player from each team competes in each round to fulfill the teacher's request. "Place the note in the third space"; "Place the note in the second space," etc. A point is awarded to the team whose player succeeds first.

Variation: Follow the same rules using lines.

Variation: Follow the same rules using note names.

WHAT AM I?

Grades: 2-4

Number of Players: Large Group

Equipment: Music Symbol Flashcards (See Appendix)

Directions:

Each child is given a different card which he puts face down on his desk. "It" stands in front and describes the symbol on his card until someone guesses correctly. The person who guesses correctly is "It" for the next round.

BEAN BAGS IN THE LINES

Grades: 2-5

Number of Players: Large Group

Equipment: Six Bean Bags (See Appendix). Floor Staff (See Appendix)

Directions:

The class is divided into two teams with one player

from each team competing in a round. A round consists of one player from each team tossing three bean bags from a designated spot. When a bean bag lands on any line a team point is awarded. The team with the most points at the end of play is the winner.

Variation: Lines may be awarded different values: F=5, D=4, B=3, G=2, E=1.

BEAN BAGS IN THE SPACES

Grades: 2-5

Number of Players: Large Group

Equipment: Six Bean Bags (See Appendix). Floor Staff (See Appendix)

Directions:

The class is divided into two teams with one player from each team competing in a round. A round consists of one player from each team tossing three bean bags from a designated spot. When a bean bag lands on any space, a team point is awarded. The team with the most points at the end of the game is the winner.

Variation: Spaces may be awarded different values: E=4, C=3, A=2, F=1.

BEAN BAG TOSS

Grades: 2-5

Number of Players: Large Group

Equipment: Four Bean Bags (See Appendix). Floor Staff (See Appendix)

Directions:

The class is divided into two teams. One player from each team competes in a round. The player, standing at a designated spot, tosses a bean bag onto the staff and names the note that belongs to the line or space where his bean bag has landed. Each player gets two tosses. One point is awarded to his team for each note correctly named. The team with the most points at the end of the game is the winner. If the bean bag does not land close to the center of the line or space, it should not be counted at all.

CAMERA

Grades: 2-5

Number of Players: Large Group

Equipment: Chalkboard staff and chalk

Directions:

Students close their eyes while the teacher writes a note on the chalkboard staff. When the teacher says "click," the students open their eyes to look at the note. The teacher immediately erases the note. Someone is called upon to "develop his film" and tell the note he saw. A correct answer earns the privilege of writing the next note.

CAN YOU FIND IT?

Grades: 2-5

Number of Players: Large Group

Equipment: Chalkboard or flannel board that has been filled with symbols during the lesson.

Directions:

The teacher asks individual students to find a certain music symbol, to remove it from the board, and then to line up at the door. In a short while, the whole class has played the game and is ready to leave the room. This is a great way to end the lesson!

FIND-THE-NOTE RELAY

Grades: 2-5

Number of Players: Small or Large Group

Equipment: Two sets of Treble Clef Note Cards (See Appendix)

Directions:

Players are divided into two teams. One player from each team competes in a round. A set of Treble Clef Note Cards may be placed at either end of a table. The player stands beside the cards and upon the signal attempts to find the card requested by the teacher (i.e., "third space C"). The first player to produce the correct card has won that round and earned a point for his team.

INTELLIGENCE TEST

Grades: 2-5

Number of Players: Small or Large Group

Equipment: Paper and pencil for each student. Directions written on the board or on a prepared spirit master

Directions:

T O   Y   I S   O O   Y.
    ‾1‾ ‾2‾   ‾3‾   ‾4‾ ‾5‾   ‾6‾ ‾7‾

Follow these directions to complete the above puzzle.

1. Write the name of this note in blanks 1, 5, 6.

2. Write the name of this note in blanks 2, 3, 7.

3. Write the name of this note in blank 4.

MUSIC HUNT

Grades: 2-5

Number of Players: Large Group

Equipment: Music Symbol Flashcards (See Appendix). Existing bulletin boards and displays

Directions:

Each student is given a card. He must find a matching symbol in the room within a certain time limit (try 4 minutes). This is the very thing to wake up a sleepy bunch!

MUSICAL SPELL-IT

Grades: 2-5

Number of Players: Small or Large Group

Equipment: Individual Flannel Boards (See Appendix). Felt Note Discs (See Appendix). Word Cards (See Appendix)

Directions:

Players are divided into teams. The teacher calls out the "spelling word" and shows its corresponding card (optional). The students "spell it" on their staff. At the end of sixty seconds each correct Flannel Board earns a team point.

AROUND THE WORLD

Grades: 2-5

Number of Players: Small or Large Group

Equipment: Primary Cards (See Appendix) or Music Symbol Flashcards (See Appendix)

Directions:

Select the cards according to the ability of the group. Players are seated in a circle. The first two players stand. The teacher holds one card in front of them. The player who is first to identify the symbol is the winner. The losing player is seated while the winner moves on down the circle to stand beside the next player. The teacher then displays another card to be identified. The object is for a player to continue winning (and moving around the circle) for as long as possible. Any player who can successfully win over every other player is said to have gone "Around the World."

NAME THE WORD

Grades: 2-5

Number of Players: Small or Large Group

Equipment: Word Cards: notated (See Appendix)

Directions:

The leader displays a card selected from the stack. The student who is first to correctly name the word is the winner. He may earn the privilege of selecting the next card.

GRAND STAFF BINGO

Grades: 2-8

Number of Players: Small or Large Group

Equipment: Playing Pieces (corn, beans, paper pieces). Grand Staff Bingo Cards (See Appendix). Grand Staff Note Cards (See Appendix)

Directions:

All players are given a Bingo Card and some playing pieces. Each player covers the notes on his card as they are called, i.e., "treble staff, second space A." The teacher displays each note as it is called. The first player to cover all five notes is the winner.

MUSICAL SPEEDWAY

Grades: 2-8

Number of Players: Small or Large Group

Equipment: Note-Value Playing Cards (See Appendix). Musical Speedway Playing Board (See Appendix). Two playing pieces (toy auto maybe!)

Directions:

Players are divided into two teams. The Playing Board is placed on a table or on the floor. The Note-Value Cards are stacked, face down, near the playing area. The first player turns up a card from the stack and moves his team's playing piece the appropriate number of spaces. Play continues with a member of the opposite team. The team that is first to reach "Finish" is the winner.

MUSICAL STORIES

Grades: 2-8

Number of Players: Individual, Small or Large Group

Equipment: Prepared sentences on chalkboard or spirit master

Directions:

Each player is instructed to de-code the following sentences:

1. We went to a little restaurant. It was a

2. We went in a

3. I ordered

4. Mom ordered

5. The meal was

6. I wished I were

Suggestion: Try using a different sentence on the board each week.

NAME-THE-NOTE RELAY

Grades: 2-8

Number of Players: Small or Large Group

Equipment: Two music flannel boards with notes, or two staffs on the chalkboard with chalk. Word Cards (See Appendix)

Directions:

Players are divided into two teams. In a prominent place the teacher displays a word that can be spelled with notes of the staff (begin with three-letter words). The teams compete using one player at a time to notate each letter as it appears in the given word. The team who has the first success is the winner of that round.

NOTE NAME CONCENTRATION

Grades: 2-8

Number of Players: Small or Large Group

Equipment: Concentration Board mounted on wall (See Appendix). Concentration Note-Name Cards (See Appendix)

Directions:

Cards are arranged in random order on the Concentration Board. Players are divided into two teams. The first player chooses a number from the board and the teacher reveals that particular card. The student then calls a second number, attempting to match the first card. The student receives one point for each card that he is able to identify and three more points if his card makes a match (five points possible total). The team that earns the most points is the winner.

TREBLE CLEF BINGO

Grades: 2-8

Number of Players: Small or Large Group

Equipment: Playing pieces (corn, beans, or paper pieces). Treble Clef Bingo Cards (See Appendix). Treble Clef Note Cards (See Appendix)

Directions:

> All players are given a Bingo Card and some playing pieces. Each player covers the notes on his card as they are called, i.e., "second line G." The caller displays the note as it is called. The first player to cover all five notes is the winner.

Suggestion: Allow at least twenty minutes for any Bingo game.

MUSICAL SPELLING

Grades: 3-5

Number of Players: Large Group

Equipment: Floor Staff (See Appendix)

Directions:

> Players are divided into groups of four. Groups participate one at a time. The teacher calls a four-letter musical word (see Word Cards in the Appendix). The group arranges themselves on the Floor Staff in the order necessary for spelling that particular word. The teacher, or an appointed time-keeper, watches the clock from the time the word is called to the point of completion. A record is kept of the time. After each group has had a turn, the winner is the group that spelled its word in the least amount of time.

WILD FISH

Grades: 3-5

Number of Players: Small Group

Equipment: Magnetic Board and Magnetic Fish (See Appendix)

Directions:

Players are divided into two teams. Each team is assigned to use one-half of the Magnetic Board. The fish are spread, face down, on a table. One musical symbol is designated as the Wild Fish. The first player begins by selecting a fish, naming the symbol that appears on it, and placing the fish on his team's board. (If he is unable to name the symbol, he does not get to keep it.) A player from the other team does likewise. Play continues in this manner until someone draws a Wild Fish which entitles that player to take one fish from the opposite team and place it on his own team's board. (Wild Fish may not be taken in this manner.) The team accumulating the most fish is the winner.

BEAN BAG TOSS

Grades: 3-6

Number of Players: Small or Large Group

Equipment: Vinyl Floor Chart (See Appendix). Four Bean Bags (See Appendix). Floor Chart Cards

Directions:

Players are divided into two teams. One player from each team is designated as the "Caller." In each round the Caller draws the top card from the stack and his teammate has two chances (give him two bean bags) to toss a bean bag onto the selected symbol, standing at a given distance from the Floor Chart. Ten points are awarded for hitting the target on the first toss. Five points are awarded if the target is hit on the second toss. The team with the most points at the end of play is the winner.

MUSIC TWISTER

Grades: 3-6

Number of Players: One at a time

Equipment: Vinyl Floor Chart. Music Twister Cards (See Appendix)

Directions

The leader chooses the top card from the deck. He calls the symbol on the card. The player locates the appropriate symbol and follows the directions as given on the card. For example, he may be asked to put his right foot on a quarter rest. Maintaining that position, he may then be asked to put his left foot on a whole note. Play continues until the player can do no more. Players in each round compete to see who can accomplish the most tasks (cards) without missing.

Variation: Have three players on the Floor Chart at the same time. Let them alternate turns. Watch the confusion!

MUSIC SYMBOL RELAY (VOCABULARY)

Grades: 3-8

Number of Players: Large Group

Equipment: Posted vocabulary list of 10-15 music symbols. Chalkboard and chalk

Directions:

The players are divided into two teams. Each team is designated to work in a certain area of the chalkboard. The teams may be lined up beside their chalkboard area or they may participate in the order of their seating arrangement. From the posted list of music symbol words, the teams compete to write the symbols, in order, upon the board (with the first player writing the first symbol listed, the second player writing the second symbol listed and so on). The team that is first to write the list correctly is the winner.

SECRET SENTENCES

Grades: 3-8

Number of Players: Small or Large Group

Equipment: Prepared papers containing several sentences that have specific words written in musical notations.

Directions:

Players are divided into groups of four. Each group works to de-code the prepared sentences. The group who finishes first is the winner.

Suggested sentences:

Do a good *deed*.	Tell your *age*!
Eat a free *egg*.	Fill a big *bag*!
Wear a happy *face*.	Turn a *deaf* ear.
Don't be a *dead* beat!	Learn to *add*.
Take a *cab*!	Get out of your *cage*.
Pay a *fee*.	Don't be a *cad*!

MUSIC SYMBOL CONCENTRATION

Grades: 4-8

Number of Players: Large Group

Equipment: Concentration Board (See Appendix). Concentration Music Symbol Cards (See Appendix)

Directions:

The class is divided into two teams. The first player chooses a number from the board and the teacher reveals that particular card. The student identifies the symbol revealed and then calls a second number, attempting to match the first symbol. One point is awarded for each symbol that is correctly identified plus three more points if the symbols match, making a total of five possible points. The team which earns the most points is the winner.

MAKING A SOUND COMPOSITION

Grades: 4-8

Number of Players: Small or Large Group

Equipment: Paper and pencil for each player. Prepared List of Sounds (See below)

Directions:

Each student is given a paper and pencil and a list of sounds. His job is to arrange the given sounds into a Sound Composition, using them in any order desired, and developing his own graphic notation. At the end of the alloted time (maybe ten minutes) students may take turns writing their Sound Compositions on the chalkboard to determine if the other players can correctly interpret the graphic notation. Considering that everyone is instructed to use exactly the same sounds, this should not be too difficult; and to see the variety of notations that arise should be an interesting experience for any group! A sample List of Sounds may be:

4 high sounds   2 wavering sounds

3 low sounds	2 gurgles
5 hissing sounds	2 sharp sounds
2 thuds	2 tinkling sounds

The entire composition should last 60 seconds.

NEWSPAPER NOTES

Grades: 4-8

Number of Players: Individual or Small Group

Equipment: Prepared story on chalkboard or spirit master

Directions:

The players complete the newspaper story by decoding the noted words. The winner is the individual or group who finishes first. (Underlined words should be written in music notation.)

"Last Saturday night a concert was held at the Beaded Cage Music Hall. The conductor was faced with a small orchestra due to an accident involving a cab full of players running into a Cafe. The accident resulted in two players dead. Another was badly defaced and another was made deaf. But the audience was very pleased with the concert and sat on the edge of their seats throughout most of the program."

PICK-A-PAIR

Grades: 4-8

Number of Players: Three to six

Equipment: Vocabulary-Symbol Playing Cards (See Appendix)

Directions:

Each player is dealt five cards; remaining cards are placed in the center. The game is played exactly like "Symbol-Match" except the "match" in this case is the symbol and the appropriate vocabulary word.

SYMBOL-MATCH

Grades: 4-8

Number of Players: Three to six

Equipment: Music Symbol Playing Cards (See Appendix)

Directions:

Each player is dealt five cards. Remaining cards are placed in the center of the table. The first player attempts to get a "match" by requesting a specific card from any player. If he is unsuccessful he must draw from the center pile. If he is again unsuccessful the play passes to the next player. If the first player is successful in securing the desired card, his turn continues until he misses. At the end of the game, the player with the most "matches" is the winner.

THREE IN A ROW: MUSIC SYMBOLS

Grades: 4-8

Number of Players: Large Group

Equipment: Paper and pencil for each player

Directions:

Each player draws a large square on his paper and marks it off into nine equal areas as shown. The leader calls out nine music symbols. Each player draws each symbol as it is called in the area of his choice. After all the symbols are drawn, the play begins.

The same symbols are called by the leader, one by one, in different order and crossed out by each player. The first player to cross out any three symbols in a straight line (horizontally, vertically, or diagonally) is the winner.

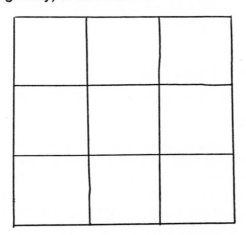

TREASURE HUNT

Grades: 4-8

Number of Players: Large Group

Equipment: A music book, paper, and pencil for each player

Directions:

Each student chooses any page in his music book. He may *not* change pages. The teacher calls out a list of music symbols. After each symbol is called, time is allowed for the students to count the number of times that particular item can be found on the page chosen. He notes the number on his paper.

After about ten items, the students are asked to add up their total score. The player with the highest number is the winner.

Suggested items: How many verses? Phrases? Half Notes? Quarter rests? Fermatas? Treble Clefs? Third Line "B"? Bar Lines? Eighth Notes? Etc.

TEAM TREASURE HUNT

Grades: 4-8

Number of Players: Large Group

Equipment: A music book for each student

Directions:

The class is divided into two teams. Everyone is assigned to the same page in his music book. The first player names any musical symbol that he can recognize on that page and earns a point for his team. Next, a player from the opposing team must name a *different* symbol to earn a point. The play goes back and forth between the teams giving each member of the class an opportunity to name a symbol that has not already been named. When a player finally cannot name a new symbol, the play becomes open to any student in the room who may earn a point by raising his hand for permission and then naming a symbol. The team with the most points is the winner.

CREATE A STORY

Grades: 5-8

Number of Players: Individual

Equipment: Prepared game sheet for each player

Directions:

The following story is given each player.

Write the correct word in the blank following each symbol.

Once upon a time there was a ♩ _____ back who got into real 𝄞 _____ . It happened in the first ♩__ of the game. He fumbled and dropped the ball pass after pass. The other players really let him know that such carelessness did not ▤ _____ up to the team's standards. The o _____ team was giving him a bad time. Play resumed for the third ♩ _____ . Our hero could feel himself growing tired. He needed a 𝄾 _____ . He asked the coach for ²/₄ _____ out. It was the best solution. Everyone is entitled, occasionally, to a 𝄞♩♩ _____ day.

MUSICAL RAILROAD SPELLING

Grades: 5-8

Number of Players: Small or Large Group

Equipment: Chalk, chalkboard, and music staff liner

Directions:

Players are divided into two teams. A music staff is drawn the length of the chalkboard. A player from Team A challenges a player from Team B by writing a word on the chalkboard in music notation. Player B must then write another word in music notation that begins with the last letter of the previous word. The game continues on a single staff across the chalkboard, thus building a "Musical Railroad." When a team cannot think of another acceptable word, they are disqualified and the remaining team is declared the winner.

PLAY THE MARKET

Grades: 6-8

Number of Players: Individual, Small or Large Groups

Equipment: Newspaper clipping of a Stock Market report. Classroom instruments (optional)

Directions:

Players are divided into small groups (two to four). Each group is assigned to make a Sound Composition utilizing the highs and lows that appear in the newspaper clipping. This may be accomplished with vocal sounds or the sounds of classroom instruments. At the end of the alloted time, each group performs its Sound Composition for the others.

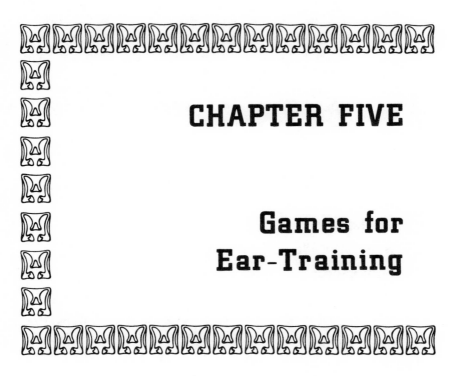

CHAPTER FIVE

Games for Ear-Training

HIGH-LOW

Grades: K-2

Number of Players: Small or Large Group

Equipment: Two resonator bells that are pitched more than an octave apart

Directions:

The two bells are given to two players. These two

players are asked to stand about ten feet apart. "It" is blindfolded and stands between the two bells. Both bells play together at the same time and the teacher tells "It" to walk toward the high (or low) sound. "It" must choose the correct sound. After a few rounds, be sure to rearrange the placement of the bells. This is a fun game for children who are old enough to enjoy blindfolds.

SHOWING SOFT AND LOUD

Grades: K-2

Number of Players: Large Group

Equipment: Drum and a beater

Directions:

The teacher plays a pattern on the drum varying the dynamic level, i.e., changing gradually from loud to soft or soft to loud. The students respond by showing hands close together when they hear soft sounds, and spreading their hands far apart as the sounds grow louder. This is an excellent two-minute activity for teaching crescendo and decrescendo.

SHUT EYES, OPEN EARS

Grades: K-2

Number of Players: Small Group

Equipment: Two resonator bells pitched more than an octave apart.

Directions:

· The two bells are given to two players who are assigned to stand about ten feet apart. The other players stand in the middle between them. The teacher (or student leader) says: "Shut eyes, open ears; and walk to the high (or low) sound." All of the players in the middle do as directed while both bells are playing continuously. The game continues with a new command. This simple game is fun for very young students.

Variation: For more advanced students, the teacher may spot students who make mistakes and ask them to drop out of the game, continuing until only one player remains. Be sure to change the bells' position as the game becomes familiar.

SOUND MATCHING: INDIVIDUAL

Grades: K-2

Number of Players: Individual

Equipment: Five pairs of Sound Cylinders (See Appendix)

Directions:

The player spreads out all the Sound Cylinders and then listens to each one individually as he finds the matching pairs. Vary the number of Sound Cylinders used in this game with the ability of the child.

SOUND MATCHING: TEAM

Grades: K-2

Number of Players: Small Group

Equipment: Sound Cylinders (See Appendix)

Directions:

The players are divided into two teams. Each player is given a single Sound Cylinder; this is carefully designed so that each pair of Sound Cylinders is divided with one Cylinder being on one team and its matching Cylinder being on the other team. The two teams stand several feet apart. Player A, holding his Sound Cylinder, walks over to the opposite team and listens, one by one, as each one of these players shakes their Sound Cylinders. When Player A finds the one that matches his own, he takes it to the teacher for a "Check." If Player A has chosen correctly, his team gains one point, and the matched pair is turned in to the teacher. If Player A has chosen incorrectly, the captured Cylinder is returned to its original owner. Play continues with a member of the opposite team visiting the team of Player A to find a matching pair of Sound Cylinders. The team that accumulates the most points is the winner of this game.

Suggestion: The number of children which may be involved in this game depends largely on the ability of the students.

STAR OR FISH?

Grades: K-2

Number of Players: Small or Large Group

Equipment: Flannel board. Felt figures of a star and a fish. A length of dark blue yarn

Directions:

The length of yarn is mounted horizontally about mid-way in the middle of the flannel board so that above the yarn represents the sky and below the yarn represents the ocean. The student is asked, individually, to listen to a pitch played or sung by the teacher. The student should determine if the tone was "high" or "low." If it were high he should place a star in the "sky." If it were low, he should place a fish in the "ocean." Younger children will be quite content to go "down the line" taking their turns. Older children may prefer to have two teams, keeping score and having a winner.

STOOP OR STRETCH

Grades: K-2

Number of Players: Small or Large Group

Equipment: Piano

Directions:

The players are instructed to listen as the teacher plays a single tone on the piano. When they hear a high sound, they should stretch high. When they hear a low sound, they should stoop low. Youngsters love this game for a "three-minute break."

WHERE IS IT?

Grades: K-2

Number of Players: Small or Large Group

Equipment: One percussion instrument

Directions:

"It" sits in a chair in front of the room with his eyes

closed. The leader strikes a percussion instrument and "It" must tell where the sound is such as, "over my head," "under my chair," "in front of me," "in back of me," or "beside me." After two or three turns, a new "It" is chosen and the game continues.

WHICH TONE IS DIFFERENT?

Grades: K-2

Number of Players: Small Group

Equipment: Two sets of resonator bells

Directions:

Three bells are displayed in front of the group. Two should be alike and one should be different. The first player taps each bell and decides which one sounds different. A correct answer might be rewarded with a paper badge that says "A Good Listener" to be taped on the dress or shirt. A new set of three bells should be displayed for each new player. This game can be made increasingly harder (closer in pitch) as the ability level increases.

Harder Variation: Have the bells hidden and have the teacher play them. Let the player identify the differents ones by calling out "One," "Two," or "Three."

WHAT IF?

Grades: K-3

Number of Players: Small or Large Group

Equipment: None

Directions:

Players are divided into small groups of about three or four. The teacher tells a silly story that beings with "What If?" After hearing the story, each group decides on sounds to accompany the story. They may choose body sounds, vocal sounds, or instrumental sounds. At the end of the alloted time, each group performs its version of the "What If?" for the others. An example of a "What If" is:

"What if you got up one morning and kicked your toe on the bed, fell downstairs, knocked over a glass of milk and slid across the floor?"

NAME THAT TUNE

Grades: K-8

Number of Players: Large Group

Equipment: Piano and list of familiar tunes, or familiar recordings

Directions:

The class may be divided into two teams. A problem is given to a member of the first team. If he responds correctly, he earns a point for his team and a new problem is given to a member of the opposite team. If the first player responds incorrectly the same question is repeated for a member of the opposite team. The problem is always, "Can you name this tune?" After listening briefly, the student responds. The winning team is the one who has the most points at the end of the game.

THREE-NOTE PROBLEMS

Grades: K-8

Number of Players: Large Group

Equipment: Piano or other melody instrument. List of about 30 songs familiar to the class

Directions:

> This game is only for the students who sit at the end of each row. In each round, the player is asked to identify a song by hearing only the first three or four notes (depending on the tune). As each student is called upon, he may keep his seat by responding correctly, or he may lose it by responding incorrectly. If he misses, his neighbor takes his place and all the people on the row move over one chair so that the first player can sit at the other end of the row. The players at the end of the rows, when the game is over, are the winners.

BEING A NOTE

Grades: 1-3

Number of Players: Small or Large Group

Equipment: Floor Staff (See Appendix)

Directions:

> Three or four children participate in each round. Each player is assigned a certain line or space on the staff. The teacher plays the matching pitch for those lines or spaces. The teacher, at the piano, plays a pattern using only the three or four designated tones. Each student stoops when he hears his tone.

BEING SOL-MI

Grades: 1-3

Number of Players: Small or Large Group

Equipment: Floor Staff (See Appendix)

Directions:

> Two children participate in each round. One is assigned to the Sol spot (second line); the other is assigned to the Mi spot (first line). The teacher plays a pattern on the piano or recorder using only these two tones. Each child stoops when he hears his tone.

GOING UP OR DOWN

Grades: 1-3

Number of Players: Large Group

Equipment: Piano or other melody instrument

Directions

> The class is divided into two teams. Each student recites individually and attempts to earn a point for his team by correctly identifying a melodic pattern as moving "up" or "down." The teacher should play the melody patterns for the students, increasing the difficulty as the students increase their competency.

HOW LOUD

Grades: 1-3

Number of Players: Large Group

Equipment: Drum and Beater

Directions:

> The student is instructed to beat the drum two times—once loud and once soft. He must decide which to play first. After his performance, a class member must guess which was played first. A correct respondent becomes "It" for the next round.

SAME OR DIFFERENT MELODIES

Grades: 1-3

Number of Players: Small or Large Group

Equipment: Piano, recorder, or other melody instrument

Directions:

> Three to five students are selected to participate in front of the class. Participating students are asked to stand side by side facing the teacher. If there is a Floor Staff, each student may be assigned to stand on one of the lines of the Staff. The students take turns listening as the teacher plays two short melodic patterns; the student's task is to tell whether the two patterns are "same" or "different." A correct response earns for the player the privilege of taking one step forward along his line. The object of the game is to see who has progressed farthest at the end of play.

THUMBS UP

Grades: 2-4

Number of Players: Large Group

Equipment: Melody Cards (See Appendix)

Directions:

> The teacher and class stand in a single circle. The teacher shows a card and sings a pattern. The students show "thumbs-up" if the teacher has sung it correctly. They show "thumbs-down" if teacher has sung it incorrectly. When the teacher catches a student in a mistake, that person must be seated. The one who stands the longest is the winner.

INTERVAL HOPSCOTCH

Grades: 2-5

Number of Players: Large Group

Equipment: Floor Staff (See Appendix)

Directions:

> Players are divided into two teams. Each player, taking turns, stands on the Floor Staff at Middle C. The teacher plays an interval on the piano beginning on Middle C. The student jumps from Middle C to the second note that was played. A correct move earns a point for the team. The team with the most points is the winner.

PASSING THROUGH MAJOR-MINOR

Grades: 2-5

Number of Players: Small or Large Group

Equipment: Resonator bells and mallets

Directions:

Bells are arranged in a major scale and a minor scale in the same key. Both of the scales and mallets should be set up behind the piano or some hidden corner. A student enters the hidden area. He chooses one of the scales and plays it. Then he must say, "I'm passing through (major or minor)." If he has named his scale correctly he may pass to the other side. If he misses, he must return to the foot of the line and await another try.

Suggestions: Have a quiet activity (reading or working a puzzle) ready for those who pass through.

PLAY A SONG BY EAR CONTEST

Grades: 2-8

Number of Players: Small or Large Group

Equipment: Diatonic bells and mallet. Piano

Directions:

The class is divided into two teams with players competing one at a time. The task of the player is to play by ear whatever tune the teacher plays on the piano. Success within thirty seconds earns a point for his team. Start with only a single phrase. Use familiar tunes like "Frère Jacques," "Twinkle, Twinkle," etc.

WHICH ONE IS DIFFERENT?

Grades: 2-8

Number of Players: Small or Large Group

Equipment: Woodblock and mallet

Directions:

Using the woodblock, the teacher plays three rhythm patterns for each student. Two of the patterns should be the same, one should be different. It is the student's problem to tell which pattern was different. He may answer with "Number One," "Number Two," or "Number Three." If he answers correctly, he stays in the same chair. If he misses, he must move to the designated "foot" of the class. This means that all players between the foot and the student who misses will move one seat closer to the "head." The student who can keep his seat at the head for the longest time is declared the winner.

Suggestion: As the skill increases, make the patterns longer and less different.

MAGIC MUSIC

Grades: 2-8

Number of Players: Large Group

Equipment: None

Directions:

One student leaves the room and the others agree on a certain object or piece of furniture in the room. When the student returns, the class begins to sing. They continue singing while "It" wanders about the room attempting to discover the secret object. The class gives him clues by singing louder as he gets closer to the secret spot. Success means that "It" gets to choose the new "It."

Suggested songs: "Oh Susannah," "Battle Hymn of the Republic," "Marching to Pretoria," "Jingle Bells."

BASEBALL

Grades: 4-8

Number of Players: Large Group

Equipment: Piano or bells. (A piano keyboard chart with names on keys may be posted.)

Directions:

The class should be divided into two baseball teams. The C Major scale should be played and sung with names or numbers several times to get the ears "warmed-up." As each player comes "up to bat" the teacher plays the tone "C" and then another tone from the scale. The "batter's" problem is to name the second tone. If he answers correctly on the first response, he has earned a home run. A correct response on the second try earns a double; a correct response on the third try earns a single, and a failure on the third try makes an "out." A team may remain "at bat" until they have three outs. The team with the most "runs" at the end of the game is the winner.

INTERVAL MATCHING CONTEST

Grades: 5-8

Number of Players: Small or Large Group

Equipment: One diatonic xylophone and mallet

Directions:

The class is divided into two teams with one player competing at a time. His task is to match with the xylophone an interval played by the teacher on the piano. Success on the first try earns a point for his team.

Variation: Name the interval, too!

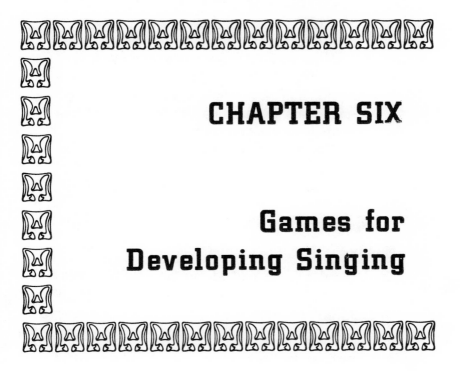

CHAPTER SIX

Games for
Developing Singing

GUESS WHO SINGS
YOUR NAME

Grades: K-2

Number of Players: Large Group

Equipment: None

Directions:

"It" stands with his back to the group while they sing

the following to the tune of "Mary Had a Little Lamb":

"Turn your back and close your eyes,
Close your eyes, close your eyes.
Turn your back and close your eyes,
And guess who sings your name."

The teacher appoints a student who sings "It's" name twice to the tune of "Sol-Mi." "It" then attempts to guess who sang the solo. Another "It" is selected and the game continues.

WHO HAS THE PENCIL?

Grades: K-2

Number of Players: Large Group

Equipment: Four or five ordinary classroom objects such as pencil, an eraser, a book, a paper, a crayon

Directions:

All players must close their eyes and put their heads down while the teacher quietly moves about the room laying the various objects on the desks of selected students. Upon completing this task, the students are instructed to quietly look up. The teacher sings, "Who has the pencil?" The selected child sings the response, "I have the pencil." The other objects are called similarly and all the students involved then get to (1) hide their object and (2) call for it as play continues.

WHO SANG THAT?

Grades: K-2

Number of Players: Large Group

Equipment: None

Directions:

"It" has his head down. The teacher selects a child to sing alone. "It" gets three chances to guess who the singer was. The singer is the new "It."

YOO-HOO

Grades: K-2

Number of Players: Large Group

Equipment: None

Directions:

Using the tonal pattern "sol-mi," the teacher sings, "Yoo-Hoo, Tommy." Tommy responds with "Yoo-Hoo, Nancy." Nancy responds by calling still another, etc. After a student has had a turn, he may put his head down to distinguish him from those who have not had a turn. The very last student gets to sing, "Yoo-Hoo, Teacher."

MAGIC WORD

Grades: K-8

Number of Players: Large Group

Equipment: None

Directions:

The leader designates a certain word in the song

which will be the "magic word." On that word, the class will always stand (if they are seated) or sit (if they are standing). It is the most fun when the designated word is one that is repeated frequently in the song.

BOUNCE A PHRASE

Grades: 1-3

Number of Players: Large Group

Equipment: Rubber Ball

Directions:

Students stand in a circle with the teacher in the middle holding the ball. The teacher begins by singing the first phrase of a familiar song. Then the teacher bounces a ball to a student who sings the second phrase of the song and bounces the ball back to the teacher. The teacher sings the next phrase and play continues. This one is a sure success!

ALPHABET ADD-ON

Grades: 1-5

Number of Players: Small or Large Group

Equipment: None

Directions:

Players are divided into groups of three or four. The groups are named "B," "C," "D," etc. (There is no

"A" group). Each group thinks of a song on a certain subject (work-songs, nursery rhymes, holiday songs). The "A" Theme is the familiar Alphabet Song; the B, C, and D Themes are created when the teacher calls a letter and the group called adds its song. In this way a Rondo may be created (A-B-A-C-A-D-A-C-A-B-A).

TELEVISION

Grades: 1-5

Number of Players: Large Group

Equipment: None

Directions:

When the teacher turns the imaginary knob to "on," the children begin singing the assigned song. When the teacher turns that same knob to "off," the children stop singing and continue thinking the song in rhythm. Several "ons" and "offs" in a song promote a high interest level and lots of fun.

FINISH THE SONG

Grades: 1-8

Number of Players: Large or Small Group

Equipment: Paper and pencil for each player

Directions:

The group sings a song. At a signal from the teacher, the singing stops. The very next word or sentence should be written by the student.

Variation: This can be used as a team game with correct responses earning points for the team! This is an excellent drill for preparing a performance.

WHO IS MY NEIGHBOR?

Grades: 2-3

Number of Players: Large Group

Equipment: None

Directions:

"It" is blindfolded and seated at the front of the class. In the chair beside him is seated the person who will sing in a disguised voice. "It" guesses who the singer is. If unsuccessful, he remains "It" and a new singer is selected. If successful, the singer becomes "It."

CHOOSE THE BEST SINGER

Grades: 2-4

Number of Players: Large Group

Equipment: None

Directions:

Players are divided into two groups. Each group is advised to select the best singer from the other group. All of the class sings together with each group watching the other. At the end of the song, each group decides on their choice and the decision is announced. The two who are selected are allowed some special privilege such as a special seat, a paper badge that says "Best Singer," the privilege of playing a triangle or whatever. This should really get your class into singing!

LINING THE LYRICS

Grades: 2-8

Number of Players: Small or Large Group

Equipment: None

Directions:

One student is "It." He sings the first line of a song and then points to someone else for line (phrase) two. If the person chosen responds correctly, "It" may continue trying until someone misses. The first person to miss becomes the new "it."

LOST LYRICS

Grades: 2-8

Number of Players: Small or Large Group

Equipment: None

Directions:

The players are divided into two teams. They decide on a familiar song to sing. Group A begins. They sing a phrase aloud and then think one phrase silently throughout the entire song. Group B then sings their song in the very same manner: singing, silence, singing, silence, etc. Singing at the wrong time is penalized. No mistakes earns five points for the team. The teacher should serve as the judge of mistakes.

WHO CAN SING
THE MOST SONGS?

Grades: 4-8

Number of Players: Large Group

Equipment: Song books or large chart with song lyrics on it

Directions:

In this game, the class is in competition with other classes, with the object being to see which class can successfully sing the most songs in a given amount of time. A Counter should be appointed and maybe a Page-turner if you are singing from a large chart. This is a terrific way to sing all those carols on the day before Christmas vacation!

CHAPTER SEVEN

Games about Composers and Music Literature

TELL THE THEME

Grades: 1-8

Number of Players: Small or Large Group

Equipment: 6-10 recordings of familiar great works

Directions:

Players are divided into two teams. The teacher

129

plays a portion of a record. Each team calls out the name of the selection. The quickest response gets a point and a new recording is played as the play continues. Don't be afraid to play the same recording several times.

THE COMPOSER BUS

Grades: 2-4

Number of Players: Small or Large Group

Equipment: About ten chairs set up in double row in bus fashion; a list of facts describing composers that the class has studied.

Directions:

The teacher reads a descriptive fact concerning a composer for each student. As the student identifies the composer correctly, he gets to ride the Composer's Bus.

Variation: Students may also identify specific compositions to ride the bus.

COMPOSER HUNT

Grades: 3-5

Number of Players: Small or Large Group

Equipment: Paper and pencil for each player. Composer Cards (See Appendix). Masking tape

Directions:

Each student has a Composer Card taped to his

back. At the signal to start, each student lists on his paper as many composers names as he can find on the backs of other players. Each student should try to keep others from seeing his card during the hunt. The student with the longest list is declared the winner.

COMPOSER MATCH

Grades: 3-5

Number of Players: Four or less

Equipment: Composer-Match Cards (See Appendix)

Directions:

Composer-Match Cards are placed face down and shuffled, being careful to cover each circle with a milk bottle cap. The first player lifts one cap and then another cap. If he reveals a match, he picks up the pair. If he does not reveal a match, he returns both caps to the playing area. Play continues with the player to his left. The winner is the player who has the most Composer-Match Cards at the end of play.

COMPOSER MATCH: INDIVIDUAL GAME

Grades: 3-5

Number of Players: Individual

Equipment: Composer-Match Cards (See Appendix)

Directions:

The player shuffles the cards around on the playing

area, being careful to cover each Composer-Match Card with a milk bottle cap. When play begins, he checks the clock; then he attempts to match all of the Composer-Match Cards as quickly as possible. There could be a class champion at this game!

COMPOSER MATCH: TEAM GAME

Grades: 3-5

Number of Players: Large Group

Equipment: Composer-Match Cards (See Appendix)

Directions:

Players are divided into two teams. The Composer-Match Cards are separated into two equal sets, and each team is assigned to use one of the sets. A player from each team competes in each round. The players take their place beside their team's cards, and the teacher calls the name of one of the composers whose name is on the cards. The student who is first to find the composer's card is the winner of the round and earns a point for his team. The team that has the most points at the end of play is the winner of the game.

ON-THE-STREET INTERVIEWS

Grades: 3-8

Number of Players: Small or Large Groups

Equipment: Tape recorder (optional)

Directions:

One student will act as the Newscaster and interview the "Man-on-the-Street." The Announcer will be discussing a specific composer, his life, his work, and his compositions. The Announcer may want to prepare some questions in advance.

WHOPPER

Grades: 3-8

Number of Players: Large Group

Equipment: None

Directions:

The players, seated in a circle, are given the name of a composer with whom they are familiar. Each player tells one fact about that composer. The statement may be true or false. If another player challenges a true statement, the challenger must leave the circle. If another player challenges a false statement, the student who stated the fact must leave. The object is to stay in the circle for as long as possible.

COMPOSERS IN RHYTHM

Grades: 4-8

Number of Players: Large Group

Equipment: None

Directions:

The class establishes the following rhythm pattern:

leg-pat   clap   snap R.   snap L. and the
X   X   X   X

pattern continues throughout the game. On the snaps the player should speak the name of a composer in rhythm, i.e. leg-pat   clap   Beethoven.
                          X   X   X X

The play moves down the row with each player naming a composer in rhythm as his turn comes. When a player misses, he should move to the designated "foot" of the class. The object is for the players to work up to the "head" of the class.

Variation: Each player may be required to name a composer not named before!

Suggestion: A list of composers on display will help some "blank" minds.

INITIAL WHO'S WHO

Grades: 4-8

Number of Players: Large Group

Equipment: None

Directions:

"It" tells the initials of a familiar composer and the group attempts to guess the name. The person who guesses correctly gets to be "It."

THREE IN A ROW: COMPOSERS

Grades: 4-8

Number of Players: Large Group

Equipment: Paper and pencil for each player

Directions:

Each player draws a large square on his paper and marks it off into nine equal areas as shown. The leader names nine composers. The player writes each name as it is called in the area of his choice. (The teacher might prefer to list the names on the chalkboard.) After all the names are written, the play begins.

These composers' names are now called by the leader, one by one, in a different order and are crossed out by each player. The first player to have any three names crossed out in a straight line (horizontally, vertically, or diagonally) is the winner.

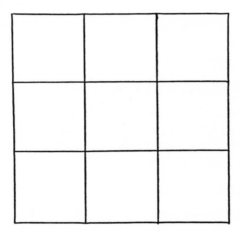

COMPOSER CLUES

Grades: 5-8

Number of Players: Individual or Small Group

Equipment: Envelope containing pieces of paper with word clues about a certain composer—a different composer for each group (or individual)

Directions:

> The player (or group of players) creates a story about a certain composer by assembling the word clues given. For more excitement have several groups busy at the same time working under a time limit. Then have each group relate its story. Reference books may be used.

Suggested Set of Clues: Bach, organ, Leipzig, Weimar, twenty, Anna Magdalena, Karl Phillip Emmanuel, Choirmaster, Germany, orchestra

COMPOSER'S CHALLENGE

Grades: 5-8

Number of Players: Large Group

Equipment: Two different chessmen. Transparency prepared with 49 squares, numbered 1-49. List of about twenty-five questions concerning a composer that the class has studied.

Directions:

> Players are divided into two teams. One player is designated from each team to move that team's chessman. Both chessmen begin at Number One. The play begins with the teacher asking each student a question concerning the designated composer. When a question is answered correctly, that team's chessman is moved ahead one space. Occasionally, the teacher may declare a more difficult question to be worth two or even three spaces on the board. The team that moves closest to forty-nine is the winner.

GOTCHA

Grades: 5-8

Number of Players: Small or Large Group

Equipment: Composer Cards (See Appendix). Paper and pencils for each player

Directions:

Each player is given a Composer Card which he attempts to keep secret from the other players. (Be sure to include the "Phoney" Card.) Upon the signal from the teacher, the players proceed to trade cards with one another. At the sound of the bell (or whatever) trading must stop and players must record the value of the Composer Card that they are holding. Round Two then proceeds with trading in the same manner as Round One. At the end of Round Three the player with the highest score is the winner. You may expect a lot of moving around in this one!

INFORMATION HUNT

Grades: 5-8

Number of Players: Small or Large Group

Equipment: Resource books. Prepared questions

Directions:

Players are divided into teams and given identical lists of questions. Answers must be located in resource materials made available by the teacher. Teams begin at the same time. The winning team is the one who answers the most questions in the shortest time.

Suggestion: Be sure that you have enough resource materials available for the number of students that you plan to involve in this.

INTERVIEW A COMPOSER

Grades: 5-8

Number of Players: Small or Large Group

Equipment: None

Directions:

One student pretends to be the composer. Another student asks him questions concerning his life and times.

Variation: The Interviewer and the Interviewee may have the class observe and guess which composer is being represented in the interview.

SCRAMBLED MUSICIANS

Grades: 5-8

Number of Players: Individual

Equipment: Paper and pencil. Prepared game sheet or list on board

Directions:

Here are some of the world's greatest composers in scrambled form. Let each player time himself to see how quickly he can unscramble the entire list. To make it a little easier, you may list the answers in another place so that the student may have a check

list. Another tip to make it easier: Capitalize the first
letter of each name.

chab	gewarn	ossau
hnusmacn	ochnip	lanedh
tozmra	venteobhe	reenibstn

Answers:

Bach	Wagner	Sousa
Schumann	Chopin	Handel
Mozart	Beethoven	Bernstein

SYMPHONY HALL

Grades: 5-8

Number of Players: 2-6

Equipment: Symphony Hall Playing Cards (See Appendix)

Directions:

Sort cards into a stack. Deal five cards to each
player. Player A tries to obtain a match of Composer
and Composition. If Player B does not have the card,
he says "Go to the Concert." Then Player A draws
from the Concert Stack. If Player B does have the
requested card, he must give it to Player A. The
winner is the player with the greatest number of sets
when all of the Concert Stack Cards are gone.

TOP HIT RECORD RELEASES

Grades: 5-8

Number of Players: Individual or Small Group

Equipment: Art supplies and paper for each player

Directions:

Each player has the task of creating a record jacket to advertise his favorite piece of great music. He must know the title, composer, and pertinent facts about the composition. One side may be an artistic concept and the other may be the written information.

CHAPTER EIGHT

Games about
Musical Instruments

SPECIAL INSTRUMENT

Grades: K-2

Number of Players: Small or Large Group

Equipment: Several different classroom instruments

Directions

    The players, standing in a circle, each have a different instrument. One player whispers into the teacher's ear which of these instruments will be the "Special Instruments," and nobody else knows. The players, keeping a steady beat, play their instruments for four beats and then they take four beats to pass the instrument to the right and to receive another instrument from the left. During this activity, the following chant may be used:

(Play) "One, two, three, four;
(Change) Now we change it."
(Play) "One two, three, four;
(Change) Now we change it."

At some point, the teacher says "Stop!" and the players "freeze" in place. At that point the "Special Instrument" is revealed. The player who is holding that instrument gets to choose the Special Instrument for the next round.

THROW IT OUT

Grades: K-2

Number of Players: Small or Large Group

Equipment: Instrument Picture Cards (See Appendix)

Directions:

The players are divided into two teams. One player from each team participates in each round. Each student, when it is his turn, is shown a set of three different instruments—two from one family group and one from another. The player's job is to indicate which of the three does not belong to the same family. A correct answer earns a point for his team.

Variation: Play the same game using Instrument Word Cards (See Appendix).

WHICH INSTRUMENT IS THIS?

Grades: K-2

Number of Players: Large Group

Equipment: Several classroom instruments

Directions:

Four familiar percussion instruments are hidden behind a screen or the piano. "It" goes behind the screen and plays one instrument. He calls on a player to identify the instrument. A correct response earns the privilege of being "It." Change the instruments about, occasionally, according to the abilities of the group.

THE CONDUCTOR SAYS

Grades: K-4

Number of Players: Large Group

Equipment: None

Directions:

This game is patterned after the popular "Simon Says." The leader is the Conductor. He says, "The Conductor says, 'Play the Violin'," and he imitates playing the violin. All of the players should do the same action. Each time that the leader begins by saying, "The Conductor says," everyone should do the motion. If the leader should omit that phrase and simply say "Play the violin"; then the players should not do the motion and any who are caught in such a mistake are out. Some instruments that are good for pantomiming are: violin, cello, bass violin, flute, clarinet, trumpet, French horn, trombone, tuba, piano, and percussion instruments of all kinds.

PICTURE PUZZLE

Grades: 1-2

Number of Players: Individual

Equipment: Instrument Pictures that have been cut-up to create a jig-saw puzzle

Directions:

Each player assembles a picture from an instrument puzzle. Pieces may be cut according to ability levels.

BLINDFOLDED PANEL

Grades: 1-3

Number of Players: Large Group

Equipment: Assorted classroom instruments

Directions:

Three students are chosen to be the Blindfolded Panel. Another child is chosen to select and play a classroom instrument. The Panel is asked to whisper to the teacher the name of the instrument played. After two turns another panel is selected.

Variation: The Blindfolded Panel identifies the chosen instrument by feeling it.

SEE AND JUMP

Grades: 1-3

Number of Players: Large Group

Equipment: Instrument Picture Cards (See Appendix). Instrument Word Cards (See Appendix)

Directions:

The picture cards are arranged in a large circle on the floor. Players and the teacher stand outside the circle; "It" stands in the center. The teacher holds all the word cards. One word card is displayed. "It" jumps from the center to a picture of the instrument indicated. "It" then chooses a new player to be "It."

Variation: Instead of word cards, the teacher may call the name of the instrument desired.

FAKE OUT

Grades: 2-4

Number of Players: Large Group

Equipment: None

Directions:

Each student chooses a musical instrument to play in pantomime. The leader plays an imaginary instrument and then changes to another. The players must change with the leader, but they must never use the same motion as the leader. A mistake puts a player out of the game.

GETTING CLOSER

Grades: 2-4

Number of Players: Two

Equipment: One Instrument Bingo Card (See Appendix).
Two playing pieces

Directions:

Each player selects in his own mind an instrument from the card. The object is to guess what instrument the other player has in his mind. Play begins with Player A placing his playing piece at any spot on the Instrument Bingo Card and asking, "Is this clarinet what you have in mind?" Player B responds with, "No, but you're getting closer." Player A leaves his playing piece at that spot and Player B takes his turn. Player B places his playing piece at any spot and asks, "Is this trumpet what you have in mind?" Player A replies, "No, but you're getting closer." Player B leaves his playing piece at that spot and play continues. In all subsequent turns the active player may move his playing piece to any adjacent square on the card, always naming the instrument pictured there, and asking, "Is this what you had in mind?" His opponent always replies, "No, but you're getting closer." Or the opponent might necessarily reply, "No, but you're getting farther," or "Yes, that is what I had in mind." The player who is first to guess what the opponent has in mind is the winner of the game.

WHAT INSTRUMENT IS THIS?

Grades: 2-4

Number of Players: Large Group

Equipment: None

Directions:

"It" stands in front of the class pretending to play an

instrument of the orchestra. He calls on students who take turns guessing which instrument it is. The student who guesses correctly becomes "It."

WHICH OF THE FAMILIES DO YOU HEAR?

Grades: 2-4

Number of Players: Large Group

Equipment: Phonograph and any recording that contains clear examples of the four families of orchestral instruments.

Directions:

The class is divided into two teams. Each player is asked to hear and identify the instrumental family from the recording. Each correct response earns a point for the team. The team with the highest score is the winner.

SPIN-AN-INSTRUMENT

Grades: 2-5

Number of Players: Small or Large Group

Equipment: Spin-An-Instrument Chart (See Appendix)

Directions:

The "Spinner" has the job of spinning the dial on the chart. The "Player" names the instrument indicated. If the Player names the instrument correctly, then he becomes the Spinner. If the Player names the instrument incorrectly, play continues with the same Spinner and a new Player.

DRAW AN INSTRUMENT

Grades: 2-5

Number of Players: Large Group

Equipment: Pencil and drawing paper for each player

Directions:

The players are divided into two teams with a Captain selected for each team. Each player's task is to draw a musical instrument of his choice. On the back of his paper, he should write the name of the instrument picture and he should identify it to no one. At the end of the allotted time, the Captains collect the papers from their respective teams. With the Captains taking turns, each one displays a drawing to his own team. A team point is awarded for each correct picture identification. The team that ends up with the highest score is declared the winner.

CLASSIFIED ADS

Grades: 3-5

Number of Players: Individual

Equipment: Prepared Game Sheet

Directions:

Each player has a prepared game sheet. His job is to guess what instrument is being described in the "Classified Ads."

Suggestions:

_____1. Lost: Musical instrument; wooden. Four strings. About three feet long. Also has bow.

_____2. Lost: Musical instrument. Small silver pipe. About eight inches long with keys attached.

_____3. Lost: Horn. Brass. Has no keys. About six feet long. Nickname, "Tailgate."

_____4. Lost: From a moving van, large musical instrument; Wooden frame. Has many black and white keys.

_____5. Found: Curious wooden tub with leather on both top and bottom.

_____6. Found: Black wooden musical instrument. About two feet long. Has keys.

_____7. Lost: Horn. Brass. Coiled tubing. Three keys.

_____8. Found: String instrument. Wooden. Six strings. About four feet long.

_____9. Found: Silver musical instrument with keys. About three feet long.

_____10. Lost: Musical instruments. Two large brass discs. Look a little like pie tins.

PICTURE-WORD MATCH

Grades: 3-4

Number of Players: Individual, Small or Large Group

Equipment: Prepared game sheet with four woodwind instrument pictures in one column and four names of the instruments in the other column

Directions:

The student matches a picture with the word by drawing a line between the two.

CHOOSE A MATCH

Grades: 3-5

Number of Players: Individual, Small or Large Group

Equipment: Prepared Game Sheet

Directions:

Circle one of the items in each row to complete the series in the row above. The first row is free!

Harp	Violin	Viola	Cello
Bassoon	Bass Violin	Contrabassoon	English Horn
Tuba	Trombone	Oboe	French Horn
Trumpet	Clarinet	Flute	Bass Clarinet
Snare Drum	Tympani	Cymbol	Saxophone
Piano	Harpsichord	Triangle	Organ

INSTRUMENT BINGO

Grades: 3-8

Number of Players: Large Group

Equipment: Playing pieces (corn, beans, pieces of paper). Instrument Bingo Cards (See Appendix)

Directions:

Each player covers the spaces on his card as they are called: "M-violin," "S-clarinet," etc. Five spaces covered in any direction makes a winner.

WHICH INSTRUMENT DO YOU HEAR?

Grades: 3-8

Number of Players: Large Group

Equipment: Any recording that contains clear examples of the distinctive instruments

Directions:

The players are divided into two teams. Each player is asked to hear and identify the instrument from the recording. Each correct response earns a point for the team. The team with the highest score is the winner.

WHO'S THE CONDUCTOR?

Grades: 3-8

Number of Players: Large Group

Equipment: None

Directions:

"It" leaves the room. The other players agree on a leader who will be the "Conductor" and each player thinks of an instrument that he will pretend to play. When "It" returns to the room, everyone begins to pantomime the playing of their chosen instrument. At a signal from the Conductor, the players must immediately change to pantomiming a different instrument. The job of "It" is to determine who is the Conductor; so the Conductor must try to be very discreet in his conducting signals. When the Conductor has been guessed, a new "It" is chosen, and play continues.

GOING TO NEW YORK

Grades: 4-8

Number of Players: Large Group

Equipment: None

Directions:

The first player says, "I am going to New York and I am going to take a violin." The second player repeats what the first player has said, and adds another instrument. As the game continues, each player names all previous instruments and adds a new one. The player who is able to remember the most is the winner. Plan at least fifteen minutes for this game!

SCRAMBLED INSTRUMENTS

Grades: 4-8

Number of Players: Individual

Equipment: Paper and pencil for each player. Prepared spirit master or list on board

Directions:

Here are some instruments in scrambled form. Each player should work to unscramble them. You might decide to have a contest and see who can finish first. To make it a little easier, you may list the answers in another place so that the students may have a check list.

| niiolv | abut | yapitmn | ratliecn | putterm |
| booe | leclo | teulf | noosabs | enobretm |

Answers:

1) violin	2) oboe	3) tuba	4) cello
5) tympani	6) flute	7) clarinet	8) bassoon
9) trumpet	10) trombone		

SPIN AND TELL

Grades: 4-8

Number of Players: Large Group

Equipment: Spin-An-Instrument Chart (See Appendix). Prepared questions (suggested below)

Directions:

The players are divided into two teams. To serve both teams there is one Spinner and one Score-keeper. The Spinner begins. The first player then names the instrument indicated. Upon naming the instrument correctly, the player has earned one point and the opportunity of earning another point for his team by answering a question from the teacher concerning the instrument indicated. The team with the highest score wins the game.

Suggested Questions: VIOLIN, VIOLA, CELLO, BASS VIOLIN

1. How many strings are on me?
2. Name two ways that I may be played.
3. Except for the strings, I am made of _____.
4. Compared to a violin (or Bass Violin) my sounds are __(higher, lower)_____.
5. The small piece of wood that holds my strings away from my body is called a _____.

FLUTE, CLARINET, SAXOPHONE, BASSOON
1. I am made of _____.
2. The sounds that I play are usually __(high, low, high & low)__.
3. To which family of instruments do I belong?
4. Am I held at the front or the side of the player's body?
5. Compared to a __(name an instrument)__, am I larger or smaller?

TRUMPET, FRENCH HORN, TROMBONE, TUBA
1. How many valves do I have?
2-5. Same as Flute 1-4.

PERCUSSION INSTRUMENTS
1. To which family of instruments do I belong?
2. Can I be tuned to more than one pitch?
3. Can I play a melody?
4. Would my tone be best described as short or long?
5. Can you name a special "sound effect" that I might be good for?

INSTRUMENT RUMMY

Grades: 5-8

Number of Players: 2-4

Equipment: Deck of Instrument Playing Cards (See Appendix)

Directions:

Each player is given five cards. The remaining cards are placed in the center of the table. The object of the game is to acquire sets of four common instruments (string, brass, woodwind, or percussion). The first player draws from the center pile. He may choose to keep the card or to discard it face up. At the end of the game, the player with the most sets is the winner.

WHAT'S THE MATTER?

Grades: 5-8

Number of Players: Individual, Small or Large Group

Equipment: Paper and pencil for each player

Directions:

Each player is assigned to draw a picture of one or more musicians playing an instrument. Each drawing should contain an error. The teacher duplicates and/or exchanges the pictures and other players can discover the errors.

Variation: Project the drawings on the Opaque Projector.

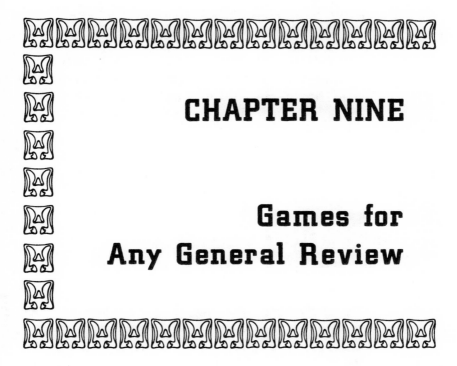

CHAPTER NINE

Games for
Any General Review

ONE-HUNDRED PER CENT

Grades: 1-4

Number of Players: Large Group

Equipment: Depends upon the adaptation

Directions:

When the teacher is fairly certain that everyone in
the class has mastered a certain skill, he may chal-

lenge the class to a game of "One-Hundred Per Cent." If everyone in the class does indeed accomplish the assigned task, then the class is the victor. If so much as one mistake is made, the teacher is the victor. This is especially good with flash card drill, echo patterns, and making notes or symbols at the chalk board. Be sure that each student performs alone.

THUMBS DOWN

Grades: 1-4

Number of Players: Large Group

Equipment: None

Directions:

The class stands in a circle around the teacher. The teacher makes declaratory statements. The students respond by showing "thumbs up" if the statement is true and "thumbs down" if the statement is false. When the teacher catches a student in a mistake, the student must sit down. Those who are standing at the end of the game are declared the winners. To make it harder the teacher may use her thumbs "up" or "down" to try to fool the students. Suggested topics: music symbols and their meanings; music literature; instruments of the orchestra.

MUSICAL SPEEDWAY: GENERAL REVIEW

Grades: 2-8

Number of Players: Small or Large Group

Equipment: Musical Speedway Playing Board (See Appendix). Two playing pieces (toy autos maybe!). Review questions prepared by the class or teacher

Directions:

Players are divided into two teams. The Playing Board is placed on a table or on the floor. The first player is asked a question by the teacher. A correct answer earns the privilege of moving his team's playing piece ahead for one space. Play passes to a member of the opposite team. The team that is first to reach "Finish" is declared the winner.

Variation: The teacher may offer more difficult "bonus questions" from time to time which may earn the privilege of moving extra spaces ahead!

QUIZ PANEL

Grades: 2-8

Number of Players: Large Group

Equipment: Prepared questions. Four chairs set in front

Directions:

The teacher asks questions of individual panel members. When a panel member misses, he chooses another student to be his replacement.

SHARK

Grades: 3-5

Number of Players: Small or Large Group

Equipment: Prepared review questions

Directions:

One player is the "Shark." The others line up side by side at one side of the playing area. The Shark asks each player a question that is worth a specific number of steps. If the player responds correctly, he takes that number of steps. If he cannot answer the question correctly, that player is out. The player who progresses farthest across the room is the winner.

TIC-TAC-TOE

Grades: 2-8

Number of Players: Large Group

Equipment: 9 chairs arranged in 3 rows of 3

Directions:

The class is divided into two teams. Problems are given alternately to each team with a different member responding in each round. Each correct response means that that player has earned the privilege of sitting in a chair on the Tic-Tac-Toe board. The winning team is the one that accomplishes a row of three, just as in the paper-pencil Tic-Tac-Toe.

Suggested Problems: Recognizing Flash Cards, Interval Identification, playing melody patterns on bells, or answering review questions.

GO TO THE HEAD OF THE CLASS

Grades: 5-8

Number of Players: Large Group

Equipment: Prepared questions and answers

Directions:

The leader asks a question of each student. If the student answers correctly, he moves ahead in the classroom from desk to desk, grade to grade. The winner is the one who gives the most correct answers.

MUSIC BASEBALL

Grades: 3-8

Number of Players: Large Group

Equipment: Prepared review questions. 4 chairs arranged as a baseball diamond

Directions:

The class is divided into two teams. One team is up to bat. Each "batter" must move to first base. He moves ahead as successive batters answer correctly. If a batter "misses" his question then the team has an "out." Three outs are allowed before the next team is "up to bat." The team that has earned the most runs at the end of play is the winner.

LIE DETECTOR

Grades: 4-8

Number of Players: Large Group

Equipment: Prepared questions and answers

Directions:

One student sits in a chair and is asked questions on a specific topic. He may answer the questions true or false. A jury of students must decide if he is correct or not.

SEES ALL-KNOWS ALL

Grades: 4-8

Number of Players: Large Group

Equipment: Prepared questions and answers

Directions:

Each student prepares a question and answer. The student reads his question and answer to the "seer." The "seer" must tell if the answer is correct. A new "seer" is chosen when a question is missed.

Suggestion: Assign the questions and answers to be prepared as homework.

SPIRIT

Grades: 4-8

Number of Players: Large Group

Equipment: Prepared questions and answers

Directions:

A student reads a question and an answer to the "spirit" (a hidden student). The "spirit" responds with "you are correct" or "you are incorrect." When the "spirit" makes a mistake, he loses his authority and a new "spirit" is selected.

PANEL OF EXPERTS

Grades: 5-8

Number of Players: Large Group

Equipment: Prepared list of questions on a specific topic

Directions:

The game starts with five volunteers who think they have all the answers. Everyone in the class makes up a question on a specific topic. The five experts sit in the front of the room while other class members ask the questions. If the expert cannot answer the question, the questioner takes his place. The five people remaining at the end of the game are the "experts." Let the class know in advance about this so that they can all be prepared to be experts.

Suggestion: Have the students prepare the questions.

SPELLING BEE

Grades: 5-8

Number of Players: Large Group

Equipment: List of vocabulary spelling words for teacher (See Appendix)

Directions:

The class is divided into two teams with the teams standing along opposite walls facing each other. The teacher calls the spelling words, progressing from easy to difficult. The students respond, one at a time, from alternate teams. Two mistakes in a word means that that student is out and must return to his chair. The person who stands the longest is the champion music speller.

Suggestion: Give out a list of spelling words a day or so before the Spelling Bee so students can prepare.

MUSIC MASTER'S TOURNAMENT

Grades: 6-8

Number of Players: Large Group

Equipment: 50 prepared questions in each of 5 different categories (instruments, composers, music symbols, music writing, music reading, music literature, singing, vocabulary). The questions should progress from easy to difficult. Any records, flashcards, etc. that are necessary for any of the questions. Red art paper for "tickets" (2" x 3"). Yellow art paper for "tickets" (2" x 3"). Blue art paper for "tickets" (2" x 3"). "First Prize Award" made from art paper. "Second Prize Award" made from art paper. "Third Prize Award" made from art paper

Directions:

In this game the classes are competing against each other. In each round the student may choose his category. Then the teacher reads the question. A correct response earns for the student a red "ticket" in Round One, a yellow "ticket" in Round Two and a blue "ticket" in Round Three. At the end of the tournament, all of the tickets are totaled according to the following: Red ticket = 1 point; Yellow ticket = 2 points; Blue ticket = 3 points. The class with the most points is declared winner of the tournament. Try this at the end of the year when the questions may cover material that has been studied throughout the year. You may want to have each Round on a different day making the Tournament last for three days.

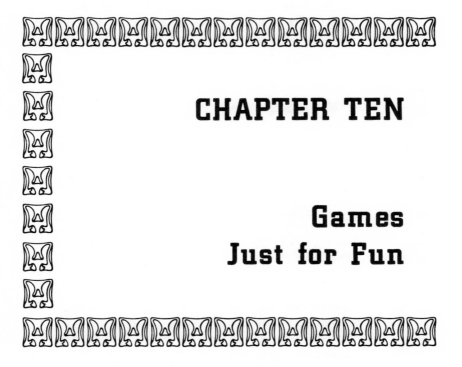

CHAPTER TEN

Games
Just for Fun

NUMBER PLEASE

Grades: 2-4

Number of Players: Individual

Equipment: One set of diatonic bells with numbers 1-8 taped on them

Directions:

The student "dials his telephone number" by playing

the appropriate bell tone. Zeros and nines should be replaced by rests.

Variation: A tune may be composed from the telephone number pattern.

Suggestion: Try one or two students per day.

MUSICAL ARITHMETIC

Grades: 3-8

Number of Players: Individual, Small or Large Group

Equipment: Chalkboard or paper and pencil for everyone

Directions:

The teacher reads arithmetic problems similar to the following. In the scoring, one point is awarded for each correct part and ten points are awarded for the correct final answer.

Take the number of strings on a violin	4
Add the number in a trio	+ 3
	7
Add the number in a quartet	+ 4
	11
Subtract the number of beats in a whole note	− 4
Final Answer	7

Suggestion: Make up problems using the following facts:

1	2	3
solo	duet	trio
quarter note	half note	dotted half note
quarter rest	half rest	number of valves on a trumpet

4	5	6
quartet	quintet	number of strings
whole note		on a guitar
whole rest		sextette
number of strings		
on a violin		

7	8	12	88
septette	octave	chords on	keys on
	octette	autoharp	piano

TWENTY QUESTIONS

Grades: 3-8

Number of Players: Large Group

Equipment: None

Directions:

"It" stands in front fo the class with a particular fact in his head—maybe a certain composer, composition or instrument. Members of the class may ask up to twenty questions as they attempt to discover what "It" is thinking of. All the questions may be answered only with "yes" or "no." Don't forget to keep count of the questions!

WHISTLING CONTEST

Grades: 3-8

Number of Players: Two at a time

Equipment: None

Directions:

> The players stand back to back. On signal, they turn, face each other and begin to whistle any song. The one that whistles the longest is the winner.

GOING TO THE ROCK CONCERT

Grades: 4-8

Number of Players: Two

Equipment: Game Sheet, die, two playing pieces

Directions:

> The path to the Rock Concert is filled with certain Accomplishments and Set-backs.
> 1. Roll a die to see how many spaces to move forward.
> 2. Move forward two extra spaces each time that you land on an "Accomplishment" space.
> 3. Move backward five spaces each time that you land on a "Lost Ticket" space.
> 4. Pass your opponent if necessary or stop beside him.
> 5. You must roll the "exact number" on the die to finally make it to the Rock Concert.

GUESS THE PATTERN

Grades: 5-8

Number of Players: Large Group

Equipment: Chalkboard and chalk

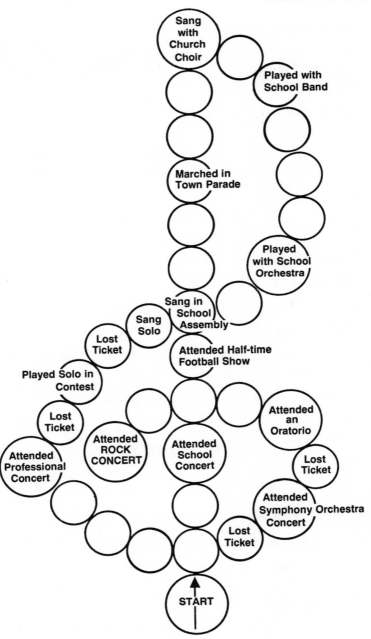

Directions:

The students study a series of musical symbols that are on the chalkboard. They attempt to guess the pattern of organization.

Suggestions:

PP	P	F
F	MF	P
moderato	allegro	vivace

MUSICAL CAREERS

Grades: 5-8

Number of Players: Large Group

Equipment: Paper and pencil for each player

Directions:

Each player writes down as many musical jobs as he can think of in five minutes.

Variation: The students illustrate each one.

PASS WORD

Grades: 5-8

Number of Players: Small Group

Equipment: Vocabulary Playing Cards (See Appendix)

Directions:

Players are divided into two teams. One player from each team receives identical cards. They alternately give one-word clues to their teammates. The first correct answer gets the point.

SERIES CIRCUITS

Grades: 5-8

Number of Players: Individual, Small or Large Group

Equipment: The problems below should be on the chalkboard or on a spirit master.

Directions:

Complete the series:

1. 𝅝 , 𝅗𝅥 , 𝅘𝅥 , ____ , _____

2. c,   d,   e,   f,   g,   __ __ __

3. ▬ , ▬ , 𝄽 , ____ _____

4. violin, viola, _____ , _____

5. 𝅘𝅥𝅯 , 𝅘𝅥𝅯 , 𝅘𝅥 , ____ , _____

6. tuba, trombone, _____ _____

7. 2/4 , 3/4 , ____ , _____

8. 𝄾 𝅘𝅥𝅮 , 𝄽 𝅘𝅥 , ▬ ____ , _____ _____

9. C   G · D   A ____ _____

10. 𝅝 𝅝 , 𝅗𝅥 𝅗𝅥 , 𝅗𝅥 ____ , _____ _____

SONG TITLE CHARADES

Grades: 5-8

Number of Players: Large Group

Equipment: None

Directions:

Players are divided into two teams. Each team has a captain. Each round consists of two halves. In each half, one player visits the opposing team to receive a song title; then the player acts out the song title for members of his own team to guess. Any of the traditional motions for charades may be used, but no speech or vocal sound is permitted. The team that guesses its song title in the shortest number of minutes is the winner of the round.

SPEAK A SENTENCE MUSICALLY

Grades: 5-8

Number of Players: Large Group

Equipment: A list of any thirty sentences. Slips of paper containing the following words: piano, forte, dimuendo, crescendo, ritardando, accelerando, allegro, andante

Directions:

Players are divided into two teams. Each student draws a word from the box, shows it to the teacher and to the opposing team. He then reads the designated sentence according to the style indicated, so that his teammates can guess which word was drawn from the box. For example, a student may have drawn the word "Andante" and the sentence, "But tomorrow is the picnic!"

Suggestion: Liven up this game by using humorous or seasonal sentences!

TELEGRAMS

Grades: 3-8

Number of Players: Individual, Small or Large Group

Equipment: Prepared game sheets, pencils

Directions:

The missing letters in the following sentences are all found in the music alphabet. Prepare the sentences on music manuscript paper, so that the student can complete the sentences by writing in the correct note.

1. MOZ_RT PL_YS _ _ON_ _RT _T TOWN H_LL.
2. _ _ _H'S WI_ _ H_S _NOTH_R_HIL_!
3. _ _ _THOV_N'S H_ _RIN_ IS _ROWIN_ WORS_ _ _ILY.
4. SOUS_ PROMOT_ _TO M_RIN_ _ _N_ _IR_ _TOR.
5. "MY_ _IR L_ _Y" H_S _ _ _OM_ _SM_SH HIT!

Answers:

1. Mozart plays a concert at Town Hall
2. Bach's wife has another child.
3. Beethoven's hearing is growing worse daily.
4. Sousa promoted to Marine Band Director.
5. "My Fair Lady" has become a smash hit!

WHERE AM I PERFORMING?

Grades: 5-8

Number of Players: Two

Equipment: Game Sheet for each player prepared with two grids—both with thirty-six squares that are lettered in one direction and numbered in another

Directions:

Each player prepares his game sheet by secretly writing the names of five concerts in five random squares on Grid I. Player A then calls a specific square, i.e., "F-Three." Player replies "hit" or "miss" and then marks that square in Grid II. Play continues with each player accumulating points for each concert that is located. The first player who locates all of his opponent's concerts is the winner.

Suggested concerts and their point values: Lincoln Center, 10; Carnegie Hall, 8; Kennedy Center, 5; Town Hall, 2; Newport Festival, 2.

CHAPTER ELEVEN

Musical
Word Games

INSTRUMENT CROSS WORD PUZZLE

Grades: 3-8

Number of Players: Individual

Equipment: Prepared Game Sheet

Directions:

Copy this puzzle for some fun.

Across

1. A group of instruments

2. The highest double reed

4. The highest string instrument

6. The highest brass instrument

8. A woodwind instrument made of brass, but played with a reed

9. The lowest of the brasses

10. The French _____

11. Percussion that can play a melody

Down

1. The lowest woodwind

3. A woodwind instrument—usually black

5. A player must sit to play this string instrument

7. A brass instrument with a slide

Solution:

Across	Down
1. band	1. bassoon
2. oboe	3. clarinet
4. violin	5. cello
6. trumpet	7. trombone
8. saxophone	
9. tuba	
10. horn	
11. bells	

HANGMAN

Grades: 3-8

Number of Players: Small or Large Group

Equipment: Chalkboard, chalk for large groups. Paper and pencil for small groups

Directions:

The leader thinks of a word and puts on the chalk-board a short line for each letter in the word. The other players take turns trying to guess the word by calling out letters. When a letter is called that belongs to the word, the hanging is begun. Scaffold

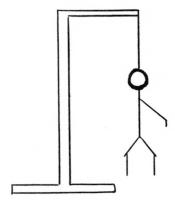

and rope should already be waiting on the chalk-board. For each wrong letter called, the hanging progresses with a head, neck, body, legs, arms, and so on.

THREE IN A ROW: MUSIC VOCABULARY

Grades: 4-8

Number of Players: Large Group

Equipment: Paper and pencil for each player

Directions:

Each player draws a large square on his paper and marks it off into nine equal areas as shown. The leader calls out nine words of musical vocabulary. Each player writes each word as it is called in the area of his choice. (Spelling doesn't count.) After all the words are written, the play begins. These words are then called by the leader, one by one, in different order and are crossed out by each player. The first player to have any three words crossed out in a straight line (horizontally, vertically, or diagonally) is the winner.

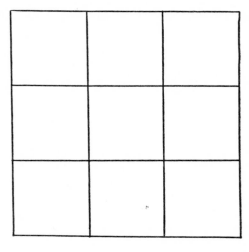

HIDDEN WORDS NO. 1

Grades: 5-8

Number of Players: Individual

Equipment: Game sheet and pencil

Directions:

Find about 30 musical words in the following puzzle. Look horizontally, vertically, and backwards.

```
E   V   I   T   A   T   I   C   E   R   S
S   A   T   O   Q   U   A   R   T   E   T
C   P   E   R   A   S   O   N   G   F   U
P   T   O   C   H   O   I   R   A   R   B
R   A   S   H   E   C   C   O   D   A   A
A   P   T   E   N   O   R   E   C   I   I
N   C   I   S   Y   M   P   H   O   N   Y
O   L   C   T   B   P   B   A   N   D   A
T   A   K   R   E   O   A   D   D   O   L
A   R   I   A   L   S   S   D   U   E   T
S   I   N   G   L   E   S   S   C   B   O
S   N   A   P   T   R   I   O   T   O   B
K   E   R   U   T   R   E   V   O   W   O
S   T   B   A   S   S   C   O   R   E   E
```

HIDDEN WORDS NO. 2

Grades: 5-8

Number of Players: Individual

Equipment: Game sheet and pencil

Directions:

Find about 25 musical words in the following puzzle. Look horizontally and vertically.

```
D A D O V I O L I N
R B A R I T O N E S
U L N B O T T A T E
M O C V L N O T E S
O W E I A B N E V U
P I C C O L O P R I
E X T L Y R I C S T
R E C I T A T I V E
E R A N T M A R C H
T U B E B A N C O T
T R O M B O N E N B
A R T H I G H A C E
T B A S S O O N E A
A G U I T A R A R T
B O W C O R N E T O
```

HIDDEN WORDS NO. 3

Grades: 5-8

Number of Players: Individual

Equipment: Game sheet and pencil

Directions:

How many words can you find hidden in the following puzzle? Look horizontally and vertically.

```
A O B O E B A R N O D A N
T O I O F A I T H G U T U
A R T W E S R E O P E R A
C C O I R S H A L F T I X
W H L O D Y O P E T U O C
V E I Q U A R T E R B B O
I S O P R A N O O H A A N
O T E N O R F L E Y L T C
L R E S O P M O D T H O E
I A R I A I U S R G D N R
N B A N D A T R U M P E T
R I N G N N E I M N O T E
R E S T C O N D U C T O R
```

MUSICAL ALPHABET

Grades: 5-8

Number of Players: Individual

Equipment: Paper and pencil for everyone

Directions:

Each player is asked to write out the alphabet from A to Z, and then to write beside each letter a musical object or musical term that begins with the same letter. The winner is the person who has the most words at the end of the alloted time.

Suggestions:

Accordion	Jingle Bells	Staff
Bassoon	Kazoos	Treble
Clef	Lines	Ukulele
Duet	Maracas	Voice
Eighth	Notes	Whole
Flute	Oboe	Xylophone
Guitar	Piano	Yodel
Half note	Quarter	Zither
Instruments	Rests	

Variation: Use the same idea to find words that may spell out any message such as HAPPY SUMMER VACATION!

MUSICAL PYRAMID

Grades: 6-8

Number of Players: Individual

Equipment: Game Sheet and pencil

Directions:

On the pyramid below, write in the correct word. The number tells you how many letters are in the word.

1. middle _____
2. do, _____ , mi
3. used between measures
4. singing alone
5. a silver woodwind instrument
6. a string instrument
7. a group of four
8. a slide _____
9. an organized group of instruments
10. singing in the style of speech
11. a period of history: 1500-1600
12. the lowest member of the woodwind family
13. an early keyboard instrument

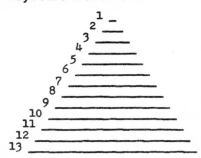

MUSICAL SCRABBLE

Grades: 5-8

Number of Players: Small Group

Equipment: A regular Scrabble game

Directions:

Play a game of regular Scrabble using only musical words.

MYSTERY WORD

Grades: 5-8

Number of Players: Individual or Small Group

Equipment: Prepared game sheet for each player or group

Directions:

Complete the following phrases to discover the Mystery Word.

1. a whole _____

2. less than a half note, but greater than an eighth note. _____

3. violin, viola, bass violin, _____

4. less than a whole note, but greater than a quarter note _____

5. a meldoy may also be called a _____

6. woodwind, string, percussion and _____

7. a conductor uses this _____

8. a keyboard instrument with pipes _____

9. they perform at half-time _____

Now take out the circle letters and find the Mystery Word.

Answers: 1. note; 2. quarter; 3. cello; 4. half; 5. tune; 6. brass; 7. baton; 8. organ; 9. band.

COMPOSER CROSS WORD PUZZLE

Grades: 6-8

Number of Players: Individual

Equipment: Prepared Game Sheet

Directions:

Copy this puzzle for a challenging activity!

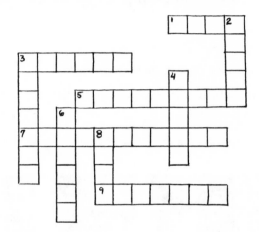

Across
1. Johann Sebastian
   _____

3. "The Wonder Child"

5. famous for his nine symphonies

7. composed "The Nutcracker Suite"

9. composed "The Moldau"

Down
2. composed "The Surprise Symphony"

3. composed "Amahl and the Night Visitors"

6. "Poet of the Piano"

8. American composer, Charles _____

Solution:

Across	Down
1. Bach	2. Haydn
3. Mozart	3. Menotti
5. Beethoven	6. Chopin
7. Tchaikowsky	8. Ives
9. Smetena	

MUSIC CROSS WORD PUZZLE

Grades: 6-8

Number of Players: Individual

Equipment: Prepared Game Sheet

Directions:

Copy the puzzle for a challenging activity!

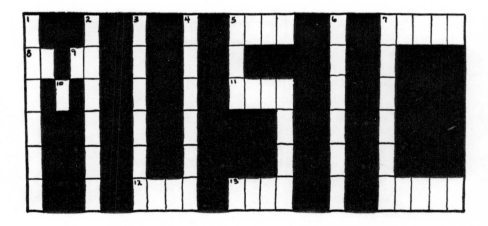

Down	Across
1. Silver woodwind instrument (Plural)	5. Vocal solo in opera or oratorio
2. Hum into it (Plural)	7. human instrument

3. "The Wonder Child"

4. Latin American gourd

5. old word for melody

6. string instrument
   (6 strings)

7. string instrument
   (4 strings)

8. sixth tone of scale

9. fourth tone of scale

10. Middle _____

11. Bottom note of a chord

12. lowest brass instrument

13. one performer

14. written on the staff
    (plural)

Solution:

Down	Across
1. flutes	5. aria
2. kazoos	7. voice
3. Mozart	8. la
4. maraca	9. fa
5. air	10. C
6. guitar	11. root
7. violin	12. tuba
	13. solo
	14. notes

TEASER-PLEASERS

Grades: 6-8

Number of Players: Small or Large Group

Equipment: None

Directions:

Have fun creating your own riddles using musical words. Use these written or oral.

Suggestions:

1. What instrument is also nicknamed the same as a kind of candy? (clarinet—licorice stick)
2. When is a fish a musical instrument? (bass)
3. When is an Indian weapon a musical instrument? (bow)
4. Why are pianos noble characters? (They are upright, square, and grand)
5. What country reminds you of the first name of a composer? (Franz Liszt)
6. Add the bottom of a dress to an insect and get a musical number sung by a church choir. (ant-hem)
7. What is a musical motto using notes names? (B# B♮ but never B♭)
8. Where do people live in London? (flat)
9. Describe a razor. (sharp)
10. What is used on a bow? (chord)
11. Name an insinuating remark. (slur)
12. Name a piece of furniture used in a store. (counter)
13. What is often passed in a school classroom? (notes)
14. What is it called when a person is at ease? (natural)
15. What one breathes? (air)
16. What an ocean wave does? (swells)
17. What is found in a jail and in music. (bars)
18. What is a part of a sentence and music? (phrase)
19. What is found on a fish and in music? (scales)
20. What is the name of a girl and a note? (grace)
21. What is another name for a cane? (staff)
22. What is denoted by a clock and in music? (time)
23. What does a policeman have that music has? (a beat)
24. What do we get at night and have in music? (a rest)
25. What does a carpenter do that we have in music? (measure)
26. What does each team do in a football game that is also in music? (a score)
27. What is a kind of tar that is also in music? (pitch)
28. What is something to a door that is found in music? (a key)

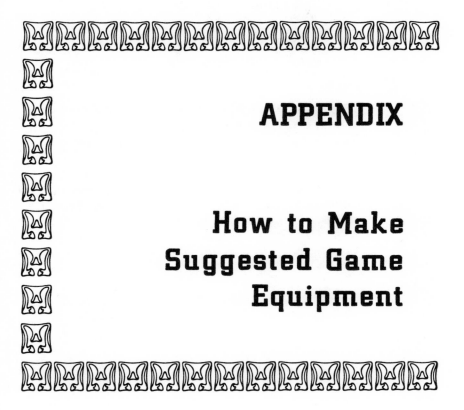

APPENDIX

How to Make Suggested Game Equipment

BEAN BAGS

Materials Needed: Black durable material
Beans

Directions:

Cut two 12″ circles for each bean bag. Sew 1/2″ seam tightly all around—leaving an opening for filling with the beans. Clip the seam. Turn inside out. Insert the beans. Sew the opening securely.

COMPOSER CARDS

Materials Needed: 31 Flash Cards
                              Marking pen

Directions:

Write one of the following names on each card with the suggested number of points in a corner (or use other names).

Bach 100	Tchaikowsky 50	Handel 25
Beethoven 75	Copland 50	Chopin 25
Mozart 75	Bernstein 25	Brahms 25
Ives 50	Rossinni 25	Grieg 25
Sousa 50	Haydn 25	Menotti 25

Make two complete sets of cards. On the remaining card should be written, "Phoney" (no points).

COMPOSER-MATCH CARDS

Materials Needed: 20 milk bottle caps
                              20 paper circles the size of the milk
                                   bottle caps
                              Fine line marking pen

Directions:

Write the names of ten familiar composers on the first ten paper circles. Write the same names on the remaining ten paper circles. In playing the game, the circles are placed inside or under the milk bottle caps.

CONCENTRATION BOARD AND CARDS

Materials Needed: Poster board
21 Pocket Envelopes (the type used in libraries work fine!).
42 cards cut to fit the pocket envelopes
Marking pen

Directions:

Glue the envelopes to the poster board in three rows of seven in each row. Mark a number on the outside of each envelope. Prepare the Symbol Cards by planning ten music symbols that will be used. Draw each of those ten symbols on two cards. On one other card write, "Wild Card." Prepare for play by inserting the cards, face down, at random into the numbered pockets.

Note-Name Cards are prepared by making a staff with a treble clef on each card, then making a pair of cards for each note on the staff. On the remaining card write "Wild Card." Prepare for play as above.

1	2	3
4	5	6
7	8	9
10	11	12
13	14	15
16	17	18
19	20	21

FLOOR CHART CARDS

Materials Needed: 16 Flash Cards
Marking pen

Directions:

Draw a different symbol on each card to correspond
to the symbols used on the Vinyl Floor Chart.

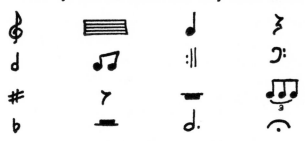

FLOOR STAFF

Materials Needed: Scotch tape #471, 2″ width, any
color

Directions:

Tape the staff onto the floor using as much length as
your room will allow. Place the lines so that there is
twelve inches of space between each line. Using the
same kind of tape, make a treble clef for the staff.
This tape is somewhat pliable, but you may find it
easier to make the curves by using smaller pieces of
tape.

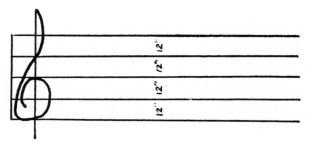

GRAND STAFF BINGO CARDS

Materials Needed: 30 cards about 8-1/2″ x 7″
Marking pen

Directions:

Draw a Grand Staff on each card. Then, on each card make a different set of five notes: two in the bass, two in the treble and one in between. Or, use some other arrangement. Be sure that each card is different.

GRAND STAFF NOTE CARDS

Materials Needed: 24 Flash Cards
Marking Pen

Directions:

Draw a Grand Staff on each card. Write a different note on each card, corresponding with every note on the Grand Staff.

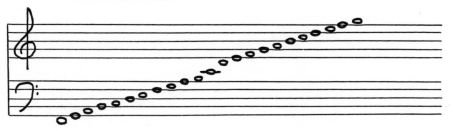

INDIVIDUAL FLANNEL BOARDS

Materials Needed: One 6″ x 10″ plywood
One 6″ x 10″ light-colored flannel
for *each* Board
Marking pen
Ruler
Black felt for note discs
Glue

Directions:

Glue the flannel to the plywood, smoothing the edges carefully. Dry thoroughly. Using the ruler and marking pen, draw a staff and a treble clef on the flannel. Use the black felt to make discs of the appropriate size to use as notes on the staff.

INSTRUMENT BINGO CARDS

Materials Needed: 30 cards about 8-1/2" x 11"
Marking pen
About 55 sets of pictures of 15 instruments—each picture about 1-1/2" square (Make them on a Spirit Master)

Directions:

At the top of each card, print the word BINGO. Under each letter, draw a column of one-and-a-half inch squares. Mark the center square "FREE." (This can all be done using a Spirit Master). Glue the pictures onto the card at random. Be sure that no two cards are alike. Laminating the finished cards is helpful. A "Caller's Set" should also be prepared by taking five pictures of each instrument used and marking each one "B," "I," "N," "G," and "O," respectively.

INSTRUMENT PICTURE CARDS

Materials Needed: 30 Flash Cards
30 magazine pictures (two each of fifteen different instruments)

Directions:

Glue a picture to each card. You should have two complete sets of fifteen pictures. Laminate if possible.

INSTRUMENT PLAYING CARDS

Materials Needed: 50 Playing Cards
Typewriter or fine point marking
pen
Five crayons

Directions:

Type, or print, the name of one of the following instruments on each card. Make two sets. Color-code the cards according to family groups. Use the five crayons to designate Woodwind, Brass, Percussion, String and Folk Instruments, respectively.

String	Woodwind	Brass
Violin	Piccolo	Trumpet
Viola	Flute	French Horn
Cello	Clarinet	Trombone
String Bass	Saxophone	Tuba
Harp	Bassoon	Baritone Horn

Percussion	Folk
Drum	Piano
Xylophone	Harmonica
Wood Block	Ukulele
Triangle	Guitar
Tympani	Banjo

INSTRUMENT WORD CARDS

Materials Needed: 30 Flash Cards
Marking pen

Directions:

On each card write the name of an instrument corresponding to the pictures appearing on the Instrument Picture Cards. Make two sets.

MAGNETIC FISH

Materials Needed: Oak tag
Marking pen
Small magnets or magnetic tape strip

Directions:

From the oak tag cut thirty fish about three inches long and two inches wide. On one side of each fish attach a small magnet. Above the magnet draw a music symbol. (Use the symbols suggested for Primary Cards, page 204 and make three sets.) The other side of the fish may be decorated, if you wish. Make a fishing pole by tying a string with a magnet to the end of a stick or ruler.

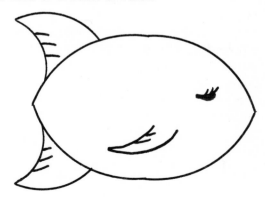

MELODY CARDS

Materials Needed: Twelve cards about 8-1/2" x 11"
                               Marking pen

Directions:

Draw a staff and a treble clef on each card. Write a
different four or five note melody on each card. Be
sure that you make three melodies ascending, three
melodies descending, and three melodies with repeated tones.

MUSICAL DOMINOES

Materials Needed: 45 playing cards
                               Fine line marking pens (Six differ-
                                    ent colors, optional)

Directions:

With a black marking pen and a ruler, mark off each
card into half, so that each half measures about
1-1/2" x 2". With the red marker draw a treble clef on
the top half of nine of the cards. With the green
marker draw a whole note on the top half of eight of
the cards; draw a whole note on the remaining half of
one of the treble clef cards. With the blue marker
draw a quarter note on the top half of seven of the
blank cards; draw a quarter note on the remaining
half of one of the treble clef cards and one of the
whole note cards. Continue in this manner to construct Domino Cards. The object is to make as many
possible combinations using these symbols. There
should be a total of forty-five cards. Using the color-
coded system helps young players.

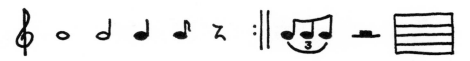

MUSICAL SPEEDWAY PLAYING BOARD

Materials Needed: 36" x 24" piece of paper, oak tag,
or colored vinyl
Marking pen

Directions:

Beginning at the edge of the material, draw a race track. Mark off the track about every two inches. Checkered flags may be used for additional decoration. Place an arrow at the Starting Line and write "Finish" at the end.

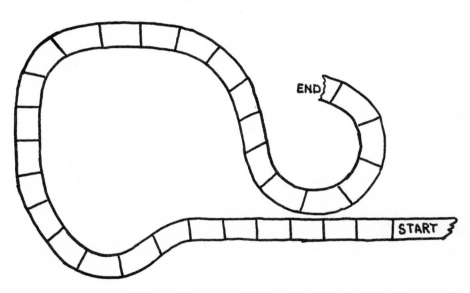

MUSIC MACRAMÉ CARDS

Materials Needed: 30 cards made of poster board
about 5-1/2" x 8-1/2"
Fine line marking pen
Hole punch

Directions:

Punch nine holes in each card as illustrated. Beside each hole, draw one of the following symbols. Be careful to make all of the cards exactly alike, placing the holes and symbols in the same places on each card.

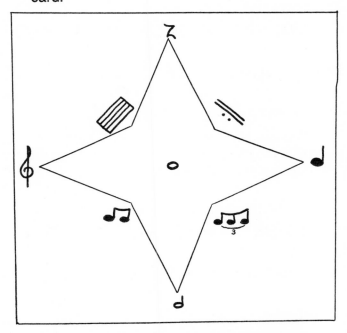

MUSIC SYMBOL BINGO CARDS

Materials Needed: 30 cards about 8-1/2" x 7"
Marking pen

Directions:

Draw a grid of sixteen squares on each card. Make four squares across and four squares down. Choose about twenty-five music symbols that will be used in your game (you might refer to Vocabulary-Symbol

Playing Cards, Appendix, page 212). Draw one of the symbols in each square on every card. Be careful to make each card different. The Caller may prepare a set of the twenty-five symbols, or he may wish to use "Vocabulary-Symbol Playing Cards."

MUSIC SYMBOL FLASH CARDS

Materials Needed: 30 Flash Cards
Marking pen

Directions:

Draw a different symbol on each card to correspond to the symbols used in Vocabulary-Symbol Playing Cards (Appendix, page 212).

MUSIC SYMBOL PLAYING CARDS

Materials Needed: 50 Playing Cards
Marking pen

Directions:

Draw a different symbol on each card to correspond with Vocabulary-Symbol Cards (Appendix page 212). Make two sets.

MUSIC TWISTER CARDS

Materials Needed: 62 Playing Cards

Directions:

Draw a symbol on each card to correspond to each

of the symbols used on the Vinyl Floor Chart. There should be four complete sets. The four pictures in each set should be labeled R.H. (Right Hand), L.H. (Left Hand), R.F. (Right Foot), and L.F. (Left Foot), respectively.

NOTE-VALUE CARDS

Materials Needed: 32 Flash Cards
Marking pen

Directions:

Draw each of the following symbols on four cards. You should have eight sets of four cards.

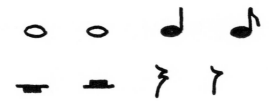

NOTE-VALUE PLAYING CARDS

Materials Needed: 52 Playing Cards
Marking pen

Directions:

Draw one of the following symbols on each card. Write the corresponding number of points in the corner. Make four sets of each card.

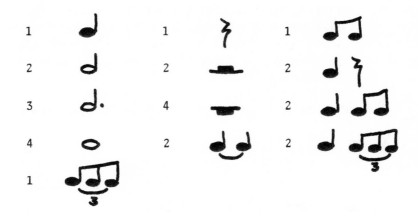

PRIMARY CARDS

Materials Needed: 30 Flash Cards
Marking pen

Directions:

Draw each of the following symbols on three cards, completing three sets of ten cards.

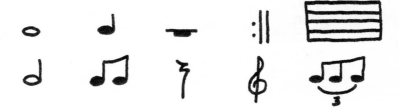

RHYTHM BLOCKS

Materials Needed: Scrap wood blocks about 3/8″ thick

Directions:

Enlist the help of a carpenter and cut the blocks to represent the note-values of eighth notes, quarter notes, half notes and whole notes. Cut the blocks about one inch wide and in various lengths proportionate to the note-values. The following lengths are suggested: one inch for eighth note, two inches for quarter notes, four inches for half notes, and eight inches for whole notes. One set of Rhythm Blocks consists of eight of the eighth-note-blocks, four of the quarter-note-blocks, two of the half-note-blocks and one of the whole-note-blocks. Make four complete sets.

Note: Actually, the blocks may be cut as long or as short as desired, provided they are in the exact proportions as above.

RHYTHM CARDS

Materials Needed: Twelve cards about 5″ x 15″
Marking pen

Directions:

On each card write a different rhythm pattern that equals four beats. For this, it is suggested that whole notes and whole rests be avoided. The level of difficulty should be determined by the abilities of each individual group.

SONG CARDS

Materials Needed: Musical theme cards (about 8″ x 22″)
Marking pen

Directions:

Draw a staff and a treble clef on each card. Choose a song; divide it into phrases. Write a separate phrase on each card. (Write the title of the song on the back side of the card.) Suggested song titles: "Oh Susannah" (six phrases), "B-I-N-G-O" (three phrases), "Clap, Clap, Clap Your Hands" (four phrases), "Twinkle, Twinkle" (three phrases), "Frère Jacque" (four phrases), "America, the Beautiful" (four phrases).

SOUND CYLINDERS

Materials Needed: 32 sturdy paper cups or tin cans
Masking tape
The following Sound Materials as desired: rice, sand, beans, pebbles, macaroni, peas, marbles, pennies, etc.
Colored markers

Directions:

Into two of the cups put a small amount of rice; into two more cups put a small amount of sand; into two more cups put a small amount of beans and so on. Continue in this manner until half of the cups contain some Sound Material. Use the remaining cups to turn upside-down over the filled cups. Fasten each Cylinder securely by wrapping masking tape around the cups at the point where they meet. On the bottom of each Sound Cylinder place a small colored dot. Use a different colored dot for each pair of Sound Cylinders so that the player may be able to check his matching ability by looking at the colored dots.

SPIN-AN-INSTRUMENT CHART

Materials Needed: Large poster board
16 pictures of different instruments
(about 3″)
Metal paper fastener and cardboard spinner

Directions:

Cut the poster board into a large circle. Glue the 16
pictures all around the perimeter of the circle. Attach
the spinner to the center. You may find it desirable to
draw lines across the circle, dividing the 16 areas.

SYMPHONY HALL PLAYING CARDS

Materials Needed: 50 Playing Cards
Typewriter or fine-point marking
pen

Directions:

On the first twenty-five cards, write the name and
number of one of the composers listed. On the other
twenty-five cards, write the title of the composition
and, again, its number.

1. Bach	1. "Little Fugue in G Minor"
2. Bartok	2. "Concerto for Orchestra"
3. Beethoven	3. "Violin Concerto in D Major"
4. Bernstein	4. "Westside Story"
5. Copland	5. "Billy the Kid Suite"
6. Debussy	6. "La Mer"
7. Dukas	7. "Sorcerer's Apprentice"
8. Dvorak	8. "New World Symphony"
9. Grieg	9. "Peer Gynt Suite"

10. Grofe	10. "Grand Canyon Suite"
11. Handel	11. "Messiah"
12. Haydn	12 "Surprise Symphony"
13. Humperdinck	13. "Hansel and Gretel"
14. Ives	14. "Three Places In New England"
15. Menotti	15. "Amahl and the Night Visitors"
16. Mozart	16. Variations on "Baa Baa Black Sheep"
17. Moussorgsky	17. "Pictures at an Exhibition"
18. Prokofiev	18. "Peter and the Wolf"
19. Rodgers	19. "Oklahoma"
20. Rossinni	20. "William Tell"
21. Saint-Saens	21. "Carnival of the Animals"
22. Smetena	22. "The Moldau"
23. Sousa	23. "The Stars and Stripes Forever"
24. Tchaikowsky	24. "The Nutcracker Suite"
25. Vaughan Williams	25. "The Wasps Suite"

TACTILE CARDS

Materials Needed: 20 Flash Cards
Pencil
Sandpaper, fine to medium grade
Scissors and glue

Directions:

Draw and cut from sandpaper two sets of the following symbols:

Glue each sandpaper symbol to a Flash Card. Dry thoroughly. There should be two complete sets of Tactile Cards with ten cards in each set.

Note: Felt may be used instead of sandpaper, in which case you may find some commercially prepared figures.

TIME SIGNATURE SPINNER

Materials Needed: Poster Board
Marking Pen
Metal paper fastener and cardboard spinner

Directions:

Cut a six-inch circle from the poster board. Mark off the circle into four equal sections. Label each section 2/4, 3/4, 4/4, and 5/4, respectively. Attach the spinner to the center.

TOSS-A-CUBE

Materials Needed: Plastic foam, or cardboard cube, 3″ to 5″ square
Marking pen

Directions:

Mark one of the following symbols on each side of the cube:

♩　　♩　　♩.　　𝅝　　𝄾

TREBLE CLEF BINGO CARDS

Materials Needed: 30 cards about 8-1/2″ x 7″
Marking pen

Directions:

Draw a staff and a treble clef on each card. On each staff write any five notes. Be sure that each card is different.

TREBLE CLEF NOTE CARDS

Materials Needed: 30 Flash Cards
Marking pen

Directions:

Draw a staff and a treble clef on each card. Write a different note on each staff, corresponding with every note on the treble staff. Make two sets.

VINYL FLOOR CHART

Materials Needed: Any color vinyl 60″ x 60″.
1″ tape of contrasting color (30′)
Marking pen

Directions:

Use the tape to make a grid of sixteen squares on the vinyl. Make each space twelve inches square. With your marking pen, draw a symbol in each square according to the following scheme.

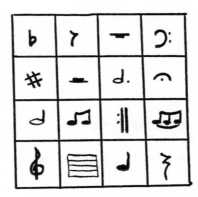

½″ = 12″

Suggestion: Sometimes the lower grades will only need the bottom half of this chart, so use an extra piece of vinyl to cover the unused part on those occasions.

VOCABULARY LIST

This list is offered as a suggested vocabulary or spelling list.

accelerando	chord	introduction	Renaissance
accent	coda	jazz	rhythm
accidental	composer	legato	ritard
accompaniment	composition	march	rondo
accompany	concert	major	round
allegro	concerto	melody	scale
andante	conductor	minor	score
aria	consonance	neumes	sequence
a tempo	decrescendo	opera	spiritual
ballad	dimuendo	oratorio	staff
ballet	dissonance	orchestra	staccato
band	duet	ostinato	suite
Baroque	dynamics	overture	symphony
baton	electronic	percussion	synthesizer
binary	experimental	phrase	tempo
canon	fugue	pizzicato	ternary
chantey	harmony	podium	triad
choir	homophonic	polyphonic	trill
choral	hymn	polytonality	trio
chorale	improvise	polyrhythmic	unison
chorus	interval	recitative	variation

VOCABULARY PLAYING CARDS

Materials Needed: 50 Playing Cards
Typewriter or fine-point marking
pen

Directions:

Type (or print) a different word on each card to correspond with the words used in the "Vocabulary-
Symbol Cards." Make two sets.

VOCABULARY-SYMBOL PLAYING CARDS

Materials Needed: 50 Playing Cards
Fine-line marking pen and/or
typewriter

Directions:

Draw a different symbol on twenty-five cards to correspond to the symbols given here. On the remaining twenty-five cards, write the names of the symbols.

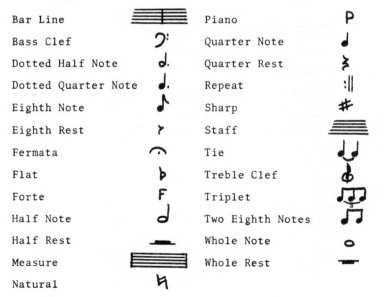

Bar Line		Piano	
Bass Clef		Quarter Note	
Dotted Half Note		Quarter Rest	
Dotted Quarter Note		Repeat	
Eighth Note		Sharp	
Eighth Rest		Staff	
Fermata		Tie	
Flat		Treble Clef	
Forte		Triplet	
Half Note		Two Eighth Notes	
Half Rest		Whole Note	
Measure		Whole Rest	
Natural			

WORD CARDS

Materials Needed: Flash Cards
Marking pen

Directions:

Write one of the following words on each card:

fag	egg	feed	bagged
fad	add	cafe	faced
bee	bed	face	adage
gag	Ada	bead	begged
ace	bag	gage	gagged
dab	ebb	beef	beaded
dad	baa	cage	decade
bad	edge	fade	cabbage
age	babe	faded	baggage
fed	deaf	badge	defaced
beg	deed	added	Ed

WORD CARDS: NOTATED

Materials Needed: Flash Cards
Marking Pen

Directions:

Write a staff and a treble clef on each card. On each card, then, write corresponding notes for one of the words listed under Word Cards (above).

Index